My only comfort in life and in death is that I, with body and soul, am not my own, but belong unto my faithful Saviour, Jesus Christ, Who, with His precious blood, has satisfied for all my sins, and delivered me from the devil and the power of death; and so preserved me that without the will of my Heavenly Father, not a hair can fall from my head; yes, that all things must be subservient to my salvation as He has given that to me in His Son, Jesus Christ. Therefore, by His Holy Spirit, He also assures me of eternal life, and makes me sincerely willing and ready, henceforth to trust Him and to live unto Him in this life, and in the next.

*The Heidelberg Catechism*

# NOT MY OWN

## *Abortion and the Marks of the Church*

Terry Schlossberg
*and*
Elizabeth Achtemeier

William B. Eerdmans Publishing Company
Grand Rapids, Michigan

© 1995 Wm. B. Eerdmans Publishing Co.
255 Jefferson Ave. S.E., Grand Rapids, Michigan 49503

Printed in the United States of America

00  99  98  97  96        7  6  5  4  3  2

ISBN  0-8028-0857-1

*In gratitude to God*
*for all of those Christian women*
*of courage and faith*
*who have caught the message of the resurrection*
*and chosen life for their children and not death.*

# Contents

# *Preface*

The original idea for this book came from a Consultation on the Church and Abortion that was held in the facilities of Princeton Theological Seminary in February of 1992. A group of pastors, lay people, and theologians from a broad spectrum of the Christian Church met together to examine the relationship between the "marks of the church" and abortion — what that relationship is and what it ought to be. By using the "marks" — the proper preaching of the Word and the right administration of the sacraments — we sought to explore how the Christian Church can respond to the moral crisis of abortion in American life.

The Consultation treated church discipline as a separate subject for discussion and so have we in this book. The decision is somewhat arbitrary but, given the general apprehension in our time about church discipline, particularly as it relates to a subject like abortion, we felt it warranted its own chapter.

Also following the lead of the Consultation, we have added a chapter on the church as servant — the diaconate — in relation to the abortion issue. Further, because questions regarding rape, incest and fetal deformity trouble Christians as they formulate their thinking about abortion, we have included an extensive discussion of those special cases. Finally, we have included an appendix, written by Thomas A. Miller, M.D., on the biological development of the unborn child, believing that accurate and current knowledge of the medical and scientific facts are important to a discussion of the church's obligation and role.

To our knowledge, no other book has approached the issue of

abortion from this perspective. We begin with the presupposition that abortion is morally wrong. We will spend some time saying why that is so, and we will respond to what we believe to be a prevailing assumption underlying the modern acceptance of abortion, even in the church. But our purpose is not primarily to provide a rationale for our position. We are not trying to delineate a new position, nor are we trying to strike a compromise. Rather, we are attempting to help the church respond to one of the most critical moral problems of our day in a way consistent with her calling.

Terry Schlossberg
Elizabeth Achtemeier

# INTRODUCTION

# *Abortion and the Marks of the Church*

This is a different kind of book about abortion. It sets the discussion in the context of the Christian Church by relating abortion to the distinguishing "marks of the church," that is, to the Word rightly preached and the sacraments rightly administered.

As reformed theologian John Richard DeWitt has written, "The marks do not define the church" — only Jesus Christ does that. But the marks describe the church, "they characterize it as an institution — they are its distinctive qualities."[1]

The Augsberg Confession, Article 7, of the Lutheran Church, describes the church as

> . . . the congregation of saints, (the assembly of all believers), in which the Gospel is rightly taught (purely preached) and the Sacraments rightly administered (according to the Gospel).[2]

And John Calvin's description was nearly identical:

> Wherever we see the word of God purely preached and heard, and

---

1. John Richard DeWitt, "The Word As a Mark of the Church" (Paper delivered at the Consultation on the Church and Abortion, Princeton, 1992), p. 1.
2. Philip Schaff, ed., *The Creeds of Christendom*, Vol. 3 (New York: Harper and Brothers, 1919), p. 11. The materials in parentheses are what Schaff considered "the most important additions to the German text."

1

the sacraments administered according to Christ's institution, there, it is not to be doubted, a church of God exists.[3]

Church discipline is discussed in connection with the sacraments in some traditions, but regarded as a third mark in others. For example, this is what we find in the Belgic Confession of 1561, chapter 29:

> The marks by which the true Church is known are these: If the pure doctrine of the gospel is preached therein; if she maintains the pure administration of the sacraments as instituted by Christ; if church discipline is exercised in the punishing of sin; in short, if all things are managed according to the pure Word of God, all things contrary thereto rejected, and Jesus Christ acknowledged as the only Head of the Church. Hereby the true Church may certainly be known, from which no man has a right to separate himself.

The marks enable us to determine whether or not the church is present. The marks do not specify what the church believes, but rather they describe how the church uniformly responds to what it believes. The marks denote action, the fruit-bearing life of believers in community. We have chosen them as a way to describe how the life of the community of believers might be expected to respond in a moral and spiritual crisis of the proportions of abortion in our time.

## Abortion: More Than a Political Issue

Abortion has become commonplace in modern America. It ends one out of almost every three pregnancies. In a single year it destroys more lives than were destroyed in all of the wars in our country's history.

Abortion arouses passions as few subjects do. It has been referred to as a new civil war; it does indeed divide families, friends and communities. And verbal sparring has sometimes regrettably given way to violent physical encounters.

Although the conflict has centered in the political arena of our society, those on both sides of the battle lines seem increasingly aware

3. *Institutes of the Christian Religion,* trans. Ford Lewis Battles (Philadelphia: The Westminster Press, 1960), 4.1.9.

2

that resolution of the conflict requires more than engaging the law. When the Supreme Court handed down its ruling on abortion in *Roe vs. Wade* in 1973, the matter was considered by many to be settled. But ensuing decades of relentless conflict have demonstrated otherwise.

The abortion debate of our time does not lend itself to political resolution. Our society has largely lost its consensus about right and wrong, good and evil, and when morality is not the basis for political decisions, power becomes the basis. All these years of conflict demonstrate that laws and power alone cannot resolve what is primarily a moral and spiritual issue. The abortion wars continue in spite of the actions of courts and legislatures because it is an issue that provokes questions about the nature of God and the meaning of life. All such issues are necessarily religious questions to which governmental answers are never final.

That is not to say that courts and legislatures have no role to play, but only that in matters of morality, civil government follows rather than leads the moral institution which is the church. While some protest that we cannot and should not legislate morality, our beliefs about what is right and what is wrong are exactly what we do legislate. We expect laws principally to protect us from wrongdoing. What is at issue today is where the standard for law comes from.

Throughout much of our history, the standard for our laws came from the teachings of the Christian Church. The Protestant and Roman Catholic founders of the original American colonies derived their moral compass from Christian faith. Today, in our increasingly pluralistic society, the Christian Church continues to exercise influence on the moral ethos of our nation. Charles Colson remarks in his book, *The Body,* that the church has not lost its influence on society, as many think; rather the nature of the influence has changed.[4] For the first time in its history the church itself is internally divided over the morality of abortion, and it now speaks in conflict with itself and with its own past, adding to the moral confusion of the country.

4. (Dallas: Word Publishing Company, 1992).

## Abortion in the Church's History

Ironically, as controversial as the subject is today in the church, abortion historically was one matter over which the church never disagreed. Orthodox scholar Alexander Webster wrote that while it is often difficult to discern the patristic conscience on modern moral questions, there is no such hermeneutical difficulty when it comes to abortion. "It is one of only several moral issues on which not one dissenting opinion has ever been expressed by the Church Fathers,"[5] and in that company Webster includes Western writers from the time of the Apostolic Fathers up through those in the period of Gregory the Great, and the Eastern Fathers during the entire Byzantine millennium (A.D. 330 to 1453). "Even a cursory reading of the patristic literature reveals a relentless campaign against the inhuman sin of abortion."[6]

One of the early church's documents, the *Didache*, which probably dates from the early second century A.D., commands, "Thou shalt not murder a child by abortion," and links the command with the second great commandment from the New Testament, "Love your neighbor as yourself."[7]

The split between the Eastern and Western Catholic churches did not affect ecclesiastical teaching on abortion. Both Rome and Constantinople warned against it. And even after the division in the church that gave birth to the Protestant Reformation there remained a unity of teaching on the preservation of the unborn. Wrote Martin Luther, ". . . those who have no regard for pregnant women and who do not spare the tender fruit are murderers and infanticides."[8] Calvin was equally emphatic:

> If it seems more horrible to kill a man in his own house than in a
> field, because a man's house is his most secure place of refuge, it

5. "An Orthodox Word on Abortion" (Paper delivered at the Consultation on The Church and Abortion, Princeton, 1992), pp. 8-9.

6. Ibid.

7. Michael Gorman, *Abortion and the Early Church* (Downers Grove, Ill.: InterVarsity Press, 1982). Interestingly, the same connection is frequently found in the later confessional documents of the church.

8. *What Luther Says: An Anthology,* compiled by Ewald M. Plass (St. Louis: Concordia Publishing House, 1959), Vol. 2, No. 2826, p. 905.

ought surely to be deemed more atrocious to destroy the unborn in the womb before it has come to light.[9]

In 1856, the General Assembly of the Presbyterian Church in the United States, true to the history of interpretation that had gone before it, expressed the broad consensus of church bodies when it said:

> [We regard] the destruction by parents of their own offspring, before birth, with abhorrence, as a crime against God and against nature; and as the frequency of such murders can no longer be concealed, we hereby warn those that are guilty of this crime that, except they repent, they cannot inherit eternal life.[10]

Both the Protestant and Catholic churches in our own century continued to warn against the practice of abortion, and numerous Protestant leaders inveighed against killing the unborn long before the practice became commonplace. For example, Dietrich Bonhoeffer wrote:

> Destruction in the mother's womb is a violation of the right to live which God has bestowed upon this nascent life. To raise the question whether we are here concerned already with a human being or not is merely to confuse the issue. The simple fact is that God certainly intended to create a human being and that this nascent human being has been deliberately deprived of his life. And that is nothing but murder.[11]

Karl Barth expressed much the same thought:

> The unborn child is from the very first a child. It is still developing and has no independent life. But it is a man [by which Barth meant

9. *Commentaries on the Four Last Books of Moses* (Grand Rapids: Eerdmans Publishing Company, 1950), pp. 41-42.

10. The Presbyterian Church felt called to issue their statement because there was a rise in the number of abortions, largely connected with children conceived by prostitutes. Marvin Olasky notes in his history of abortion that Christians were effective in stemming the rising tide of abortions, not by pressing for legislation, but by offering ministries to women. See Marvin Olasky, "Victorian Secret," *Policy Review* (Washington D.C.: The Heritage Foundation, Spring 1992).

11. *Ethics,* trans. Neville Horton Smith (New York: Macmillan, 1955), p. 131.

a human] and not a thing, nor a mere part of the mother's body. . . . He who destroys germinating life kills a man. . . . The fact that a definite NO must be the presupposition of further discussion cannot be contested, least of all today.[12]

And Helmut Thielicke, in his *Ethics of Sex,* concurred with Barth and Bonhoeffer:

The fetus has its own autonomous life, which, despite all its reciprocal relationship to the maternal organism, is more than a mere part of this organism and possesses a certain independence. . . . These elementary biological facts should be sufficient to establish its status as a human being. . . . This makes it clear that here it is not a question — as it is in the case of contraception — whether the proffered gift can be responsibly accepted, but rather whether an already bestowed gift can be spurned, whether one dares to brush aside the arm of God after this arm has already been outstretched.[13]

Only in recent decades has abortion been regarded with ambivalence in some quarters of the Christian Church in the United States. Reflecting a reversal of conviction, mainline denominations issue statements which support abortion as an acceptable moral decision or which throw abortion into a great moral grey area where circumstances determine ethical options and where only the individual woman can decide whether abortion is right or wrong for her.

But such statements issued by the denominations do not reflect a new consensus. The current division over abortion in our society is mirrored in the church. Not only do the positions taken by some denominations oppose those of others, the division runs deep within the mainline denominations themselves.

12. *Church Dogmatics,* trans. G. W. Bromiley and T. F. Torrance (Edinburgh: T. & T. Clark, 1961), 4.3, pp. 415-417.

13. (New York: Harpers, 1964), pp. 227-228. See also Paul Ramsey, *Ethics at the Edges of Life* (New Haven: Yale University Press, 1978).

# The Centrality of the Subject

The heat generated by the abortion issue in our culture has led many pastors and lay people to consider it an inappropriate subject for the church. They believe that discussing abortion is like deliberately setting a torch to the church because, in their minds, it divides believers and diverts their attention from the primary role of the church to preach the gospel, pastor the sheep and teach the faith. "Let us put this abortion debate behind us," urged the wife of one pastor, "and get back to what the church is supposed to be doing."

That is sheer blindness to what is happening, because abortion expresses our society's increasing cheapening of and careless disregard for human life. And the slippery slope, which years ago was only prophesied, has become a reality. When we read the newspapers these days, we find stories about euthanasia and assisted suicide; about withdrawing medical care from the elderly and other supposedly unproductive members of our society; about teenage murderers who are given slaps on the wrist and turned back onto the streets. A person can be killed in any one of our big cities just because someone wants the sneakers or the new jacket he or she is wearing. And an unborn child can be killed in the womb because that child's presence interferes with someone's independence or interrupts a student's plans for the future. The church is under orders to care about human life — to care about those created by God in his own image, those for whom Christ gave his own life — and to communicate the Christian valuation of those lives to the culture in a way that utterly resists the cheapening of life.

Far from being a peripheral matter for the church, abortion concerns the very foundations of our faith. And when church members face the possibility of abortion, they are facing questions of how Christian faith affects their lives. The fear of division that produces silence in the pulpit and inaction in the pews withholds help from the men and women who daily are making decisions that determine the future of their unborn children.

The issue of abortion concerns the basic characteristics that make the church the church — the Word rightly preached and the sacraments rightly administered. Only where those characteristics are found can we claim to be the church of Jesus Christ. The church's

7

stance toward abortion can undermine or underscore those distinguishing marks and thus undermine or underscore the identity of the church itself.

The Christian Church has always been summoned by its Lord to be a light shining in the darkness, a city set on a hill, the salt that gives life its saving savor. And that summons concerns the church's response to abortion as much as any other aspect of the church's life. Our continual prayer, therefore, is that the church will fulfill the role to which it has been called, exhibiting the marks of the true church of Jesus Christ our Lord.

# CHAPTER 1

# *Not Our Own*

Perhaps the central claim of those who favor abortion is found in the slogan, "My body is my own." And that claim has confused a large number of people as they have thought about abortion. Said one young woman who looked with disfavor on abortion but did not see how she could argue with another woman's approval of it, "Well, after all, that is true. My body does belong to me." Before we discuss the marks of the church, we therefore need to examine abortion's slogan in the context of both our culture and our Christian faith.

## The Cultural Context

It is now a truism in this country that the autonomous individual is supreme. Numerous sociological studies have confirmed the fact (cf. for example, Robert Bellah, et al., *Habits of the Heart*). Indeed, the highest goal in our society is to be a self-fulfilling, self-governing, autonomous and independent self. It is a sin, according to some ideological feminists, to be dependent on someone else, just as it is admirable, in the eyes of some males, to be a rugged individualist. The individual's well-being, the individual's rights, the individual's happiness and independence — those are the most important goods to be protected and nurtured in the United States of the present, and not a few of our laws and organizations are geared to such protection and nurture.

That the arguments for abortion reflect such views is therefore not surprising. Legally, the right to abortion has been based on the right of the individual to privacy, protected from the intrusion of government

9

into the privileged sphere of sexuality and conception. "My body is my own," runs the reasoning, so "keep out of my private life."

We are told that the individual has the right to decide for herself what is right or wrong and the sole responsibility for determining her own future. Consequently, we have no right to judge another person's actions; to do so is unjustly to impose an out-dated "middle-class morality" on another human being. Rather, the proper attitude is to be "inclusive," to deem all persons as worthy of approval, and to grant them the freedom to be and to do whatever they judge to be proper. Indeed, the highest good is to be "compassionate." If a woman's life-style or future is going to be seriously altered or upset by an unwanted pregnancy, and she wishes to abort her child, then "compassion" dictates that we aid her in achieving that goal. The individual's will, ethic, plans, and security are the most important goods to be considered.

In fostering such views with regard to abortion, we have of course removed the individual pregnant woman from all context of community. She is looked upon as a "free-floating," autonomous individual with no connection or responsibility to the father of the child or to the community in which she lives. There is no legal or social authority supreme above her own will. There is no natural right given to her unborn child. There is no religious authority ruling over her. She is released from all demands of family, society, tradition, law and religion, and allowed to pursue her "choice" solely on her own.

In so elevating the autonomous individual to supremacy and separating her from all communal obligations, however, we have also rendered her practically helpless to do anything other than abort her child. For we have conveyed to her the notion that we are *all* autonomous individuals, with no responsibility for one another. In short, we have destroyed the very nature of community itself.

We often hear the argument in our society that it is far better for some children to be aborted than to be born into a situation where they are unwanted or where they will be abused and perhaps starved to death. But the implication of that argument is that *we* autonomous individuals, who make up our society, will take no responsibility for such children. They are not our problem. They would upset *our* lifestyle and plans. They would interfere with *our* independence and well-being. And so better to kill them in the womb than to let them come forth into light. As one church woman remarked, "Maybe you want to raise all those

10

unwanted babies. I don't. That's why I'm pro-choice." When it comes to the question of abortion, our autonomous individualism has turned us all into a nation of independent selves, with no communal obligations and with no responsibilities toward one another.

Many factors in our society have fostered this kind of irresponsible individualism. The rejection of all traditional authorities in the 1960s and the sexual revolution; the claim of the ideological feminist movement that a woman's experience is the sole arbiter of all truth; the drive for individual material success and well-being; the expectation of comfort and a high standard of living; the overwhelming concern for youth, physical fitness, and the body beautiful — all have elevated concern for the individual above all concern for others.

## The Captivity of the Church to Culture

At the same time that the individual has been made all-important, there has been a systematic attempt, through the efforts of the American Civil Liberties Union and others, to remove the symbols and teachings of religion from every area of public life, so that no transcendent authority stands above the supreme Individual. Indeed, much of religion itself has turned to the therapeutic maintenance of the individual's well-being. "Guilt" has become a dirty word for many people. Responsibility to an objective truth or demand beyond one's own ways and reason is discredited. And individual experience, of whatever immanental or transcendent nature, becomes the one authority for all faith and action. Thus God can be defined in a multiplicity of ways. All paths can lead to the divine. All are acceptable. And all persons are to be included in any association of individuals that calls itself a church. "God has created us with our own individualities and our own differences," proclaims one document that was circulated throughout the Presbyterian Church (USA) in 1993. "We are called to inclusivity."[1] Diversity and inclusivity, championing individualism, have become central characteristics of the church.

1. *A Declaration of Conscience:* a statement adopted by the Board of Directors of the Presbyterian Health, Education, and Welfare Assocation, an organization affiliated with the Presbyterian Church (USA), 1993.

The church's theological task, then, is said to be that of "conversation," and that is largely what the mainline churches have practiced with respect to abortion. John P. Burgess has described it this way:

> People from different backgrounds and perspectives agree to listen to each other, learn from each other, and keep the conversation going. There is no need for winners or losers. If conflict arises, the rules of conversation, not of doctrine, should ensure a faithful and fair outcome.[2]

In other words, all viewpoints concerning abortion are acceptable and are to be respected, because all are expressions of the supreme Individual.

When the authority of the individual is elevated above the authority of God, and indeed, when the individual is free to define who God is and what God wants, then one of two outcomes is almost inevitable. The first is moral nihilism. As Robert W. Jenson points out, such a situation issues not merely in moral confusion. Rather, it issues in

> the deliberate affirmation of moral positions incompatible with each other and perceived to be incompatible. That is, it is nihilism, the rejection of moral argument as such. This phenomenon is not a blunder of ethical reasoning; it is the rejection of the possibility of ethics, of reasoned discourse about what is to be done. It is not a mistaken judgment between right and wrong; it is rejection of the distinction, of the possibility of asserting that one thing is right and another wrong.[3]

In short, there is no right or wrong about abortion, because every individual constructs her own ethic. Or as Dostoevsky has put it, "If there is no God, everything is permissable."

Secondly, if the autonomous individual is elevated to a position of authority above that of God, then, in the political sphere, a possible outcome is fascism, "the political condition in which it is affirmed that

2. "Conversation, Conviction, and the Presbyterian Identity Crisis," *The Christian Century* (February 24, 1993), p. 206.

3. "The Church, the Word, and the Problem of Abortion" (Paper delivered at the Consultation on The Church and Abortion, Princeton, 1992).

the rules by which we live together have no basis in real distinction of right and wrong, so that we must make them up ourselves."[4] And inevitably, the strong individual, who can rule others by the politics of power, becomes the one who determines individual and societal life.

The Bible knows all about our attempts to deify the individual. In the story of the Garden of Eden in chapter 3 of Genesis, the serpent places exactly that temptation before the woman. Come, "you will be like God, knowing good and evil," he tells her (v. 5). In short, she can determine her own right and wrong, and shape and plan her own future accordingly. Elsewhere, the king of Babylon is denounced for having said in his heart, "I will ascend above the clouds, I will make myself like the Most High" (Isaiah 14:13-14). The individual's attempt to replace God, finding its individual form in nihilism and its corporate form in fascism, is the perennial fruit of human sinfulness.

## The Emptiness of Individualism

Perhaps the most extreme view of individualism as it relates to the subject of abortion is expressed by Germaine Greer, who argues that the individual is an autonomous product of nature who, by sheer will to power, must manage to exist in the midst of a cold, cruel world of struggle and indifference. Abortion is natural in such a world, she insists. Human life merely individuates for a brief span and then dissipates again. And induced abortion is one tool given us to combat the uncaring forces of life and death and to improve the quality of the few years given us.[5]

Our first reaction to views such as Greer's is that they represent a very lonely philosophy, one that acknowledges nothing and no one beyond itself — no God, no Creator and Judge, no beloved community of the church, no forgiveness, no need for redemption. It is the same philosophy as that spoken by a character in one of John Osborne's plays: "Here we are, we're alone in the universe," she says. "There's no

4. Ibid.
5. Germaine Greer. *Sex and Destiny: The Politics of Human Fertility* (New York: Harper Colophon Books, 1984).

God, it just seems that it all began by something as simple as sunlight striking a piece of rock. And here we are. We've only got ourselves. Somehow, we've just got to make a go of it."[6]

So try to make a go of it we do. And the evidence suggests that, left to our own devices, we human beings are capable of marvelous creations — of art and music, architecture and literature, scholarship and learning, friendships and deep passions and loves. Even the most godless woman cuddles her infant to her breast in overwhelming mother-love.

Yet, how prone we are to distort or destroy all those marvelous gifts. Our vast skills turn into instruments for outdoing the competition or for devising better ways to kill one another. Our art and literature become outlets for obscenity, pornography, trash. Our friendships and loves are betrayed by indifference, faithlessness, selfishness. And try as we will to find joy in it all, we are haunted by our insecurities — anxiously restless in our beds at night until perhaps the Sominex pill gives a troubled sleep. The good that we would do, we too frequently do not do, and we cry out in our captivity to evil, "Wretched one that I am! Who will deliver me from this body of death?" (Rom. 7:24 NRSV).

For death does come inexorably, inevitably to the autonomous individual. A couple of years ago, Elizabeth's husband built a new dock for their boat at their summer place, and when it was done, they both agreed that it would last the rest of their lifetimes. After all, the old one had lasted twenty years. But as Elizabeth thought about that, it came as something of a shock, for she suddenly realized that the rest of her lifespan could be measured in terms of a wooden berth for boats. Death approaches, inevitably, inexorably. And if we are autonomous, self-governing individuals, unconnected to any lasting goal or purpose, then we cannot help wondering what has been the point of it all. Our little labors and loves and lives will trickle out and disappear. No one a generation or two from now will remember or really care that we were here. And our tombstone in the cemetery will be simply a troublesome obstacle for the caretaker to mow around. "All flesh is grass, and all its beauty is like the flower of the field. The grass withers, the flower fades . . . surely the people is grass" (Isa. 40:6-7). Yes, it is a

6. The character Jean in *The Entertainer,* by John Osborne (New York: Penguin Books, 1958). Number Twelve, p. 85.

lonely philosophy that autonomous self-governing individuals have constructed for themselves.

## The Biblical Good News

Over against the empty desolation of individualism that undergirds abortion, however, the Bible sets a different announcement about the nature of human life, and that announcement is indeed good news. First of all, in the biblical world-view, there is no such thing as an autonomous individual. Rather, in its very first pages, the Bible proclaims that we are all made by God in his image (Gen. 1:26-27) and that we can therefore never fully be understood except in relation to our Creator. Psychology, sociology, economics, medicine, art, every branch of the humanities and of science may describe our humanity, but unless our relationship to God is included in that description, we have not been fully and accurately described. We were created to live in relationship with our Maker, and that relationship is an integral part of our humanity.

Further, there is no way we can escape our relationship with God. We may corrupt the relationship or foster it, deny it or accept it, nurture it as a relationship of love or turn it into a relationship of enmity and wrath. But God is there, and we cannot get rid of him.

> Whither shall I go from thy Spirit?
> Or whither shall I flee from thy presence?
> If I ascend to heaven, thou art there!
> If I make my bed in Sheol, thou art there!
>
> (Ps. 139:7-8)

We may beg God to leave us alone, as Job begged:

> How long wilt thou not look away from me,
> nor let me alone till I swallow my spittle?
>
> (Job 7:19)

But we human beings have always to do with the God in whose image we are made. That is an ineradicable part of our being. Therefore, every debate about the issue of abortion must include that ineradicable relationship to our Maker, or the debate is not dealing with reality.

Second, the amazing proclamation of the biblical faith is that this God, to whom we are so irrevocably tied by being made in his image, is not uncaring Tyrant or unfathomable Void, all-absorbing Spirit or unconcerned Benevolence. Rather he is incomparable Love, who has revealed himself to us through his chosen people Israel and supremely in the life, death, and resurrection of his Son Jesus Christ. We can know our Maker and enter into loving relation with him as his beloved children, experiencing his mercy and guidance and finding joy and life abundant in his daily sustenance and accompaniment of us. In other words, we have a gospel to fight abortion and its lonely claim that we are just our own. For the gospel says, we are not our own! Thanks be to the God and Father of our Lord Jesus Christ, we are not our own!

We are not meaningless little accidents of evolution, interrupting the flow of centuries, destined to appear and then disappear, with no significance. No, we are the planned creations of a loving God, who has an eternal purpose for us.

We are not stumbling, erring little actors on the stage of time, burdened ever more heavily by the guilt we accumulate. No, in Christ we are the forgiven, loved, reconciled, redeemed children of a heavenly Father, who has lifted the burden from our backs by sending his Son to carry it all in the shape of a cross.

We are not dying deities, who must run the world by ourselves, only to wither and become dust in a final grave — our plans, our hopes, our dreams reduced to nought but equal dust. No, we are creations, creatures of a Creator of life, who wills only life for us, and who gives us that life in his Son, guiding our feet by his accompanying Spirit and preparing us for eternity in the company of that risen Son.

We are not lonely, isolated, self-enclosed little egos, turned in upon ourselves, whose neighbors and whose unborn children are but an obstacle to our own self-fulfillment. No, as the Body of Christ we are valued participants in a beloved community, headed by a Lord who has eradicated the barriers of sin and death that would separate us from one another, and who has given us the power by his Spirit to care and to love all of his children.

The Christian Church has a marvelous message — a miraculous message — given to it alone. And it has been empowered by the Spirit of Christ to carry that message to every hamlet and town and city and

16

nation, to the very ends of the earth. Indeed, that is the church's commission:

> Go therefore and make disciples of all nations, baptizing them in the name of the Father and of the Son and of the Holy Spirit, teaching them to observe all that I have commanded you; and lo, I am with you always, to the close of the age. (Matthew 28:19-20)

> You shall be my witnesses in Jerusalem and in all Judea and Samaria and to the end of the earth. (Acts 1:8)

The Christian Church is the instrument God has chosen to proclaim the glad news that we are not our own!

# CHAPTER 2

# *The Word Rightly Preached*

The Christian Church can fulfill its mission of telling the world that we are not our own and therefore not subject to nihilism and emptiness only if the church itself lives and has its being in the God-met world of its Scripture.

From the very first, as evidenced in the Apostles' Creed, the church has based its faith on the story contained in the Bible, and it has continued ever since, in its confessions of faith, to affirm that the Scriptures are its one authority for faith and practice.

> As we believe and confess the Scriptures of God sufficient to instruct and make perfect the man of God, so do we affirm and avow their authority to be from God, and not to depend on men or angels. We affirm, therefore, that those who say the Scriptures have no authority save that which they have received from the Kirk are blasphemous against God and injurious to the true Kirk. . . . (*The Scots Confession*, 1560)

> Holy Scripture containeth all things necessary to salvation; so that whatsoever is not read therein, nor may be proved thereby, is not to be required of any man, that it should be believed as an article of faith, or be thought requisite or necessary to salvation. (*The Thirty-nine Articles* of the English Reformation, 1563; *The Twenty-five Articles* of Methodism, 1784)

> The authority of the holy Scripture, for which it ought to be believed and obeyed, dependeth not upon the testimony of any man or church, but wholly upon God (who is truth itself), the Author

thereof; and therefore it is to be received, because it is the Word of God. (*The Westminster Confession of Faith*, 1646)

The sole authority for faith and practice among Baptists is the Scriptures of the Old and New Testaments. (Southern Baptist Convention, 1925)

Jesus Christ, *as he is testified to us in the holy Scripture* [emphasis ours] is the one Word of God, whom we are to hear, whom we are to trust and obey in life and in death. (*The Barmen Declaration*, 1934)

## The Loss of Scriptural Authority

Unfortunately in our time, there is a widespread movement throughout the mainline churches to devalue the authority of Scripture as the one rule for faith and practice, and such devaluation has taken many forms.

First, there has been the scholarly inclination to view the historical-critical study of the Bible as sufficient *in itself.* Certainly such study — with its multiple and marvelous tools of text, form, literary, and redaction criticism, of comparative history, religion and geography, of linguistics and archaeology, of anthropology and sociology — has contributed enormously to an understanding of the contents of the Scriptures. But insofar as such criticism has stopped there, and never gone on to ask after the canonical meaning of the Bible as the foundation for faith in God, it has given the impression that the Scriptures are one more interesting historical document, to be studied but never believed.

Building on that historical-critical indifference, ideological feminist scholars such as Elizabeth Fiorenza have then judged the Scriptures to be the products totally of their patriarchal environment, authors, and interpreters. Thus, such feminists approach the Scriptures with a "hermeneutics of suspicion," judging any of their content to be authoritative only if it conforms to the subjective and experiential views of modernist, "oppressed" females in religious groups identified as Womenchurch. In short, the experience of such females has been made the judge of and authority over the biblical text.

This ideological abrogation to the feminist reader herself of supreme authority above the Word of God has further led such feminists to a thoroughgoing revision of the biblical text, founded not on textual and manuscript evidence, but solely on subjective judgments as to what will further the ideological feminist cause (cf. the *Inclusive Language Lectionary*).[1]

Once contemporary human experience is made the arbiter of what is authoritative in the Bible, however, all sorts of other contemporary understandings can be imposed on the biblical text, from any branch of modern learning; we often hear someone reject biblical faith with the statement, "We know much more than that now." Thus, a popular modern view concerning human sexuality, or concerning the value of human life or the morality of abortion, becomes the superceding authority over that of the Bible, which is then seen as relevant only to its own historical time. The Bible is no longer considered the ultimate authority for faith and practice, but only a "unique" authority, that is, one authority among others and not necessarily superior to them.

Worst of all, when human experience or learning is allowed to judge rather than to be judged by the Bible, then finally the authority of the Scriptures is lost to a thoroughgoing deconstructionism, that is, lost to the view that there is no objective truth whatsoever that speaks through the text. Rather the meaning of the text is imposed upon it solely by its interpreter, and the text can therefore have any meaning that the interpreter wishes to bring to it.

Such deconstruction can occur through the subtleties of various interpretive methods, and sometimes the Scripture loses its authority in spite of good intentions. Bible study groups that ask, "What does the passage mean to you?" before asking, "What does the passage mean in its own context?" encourage a deconstructionist approach that makes it easy for would-be students of Scripture to miss the plain meaning of the text and to substitute for it their own subjective or hoped-for meaning.

There is no acknowledgement in a deconstructionist approach

1. Published by the National Council of Churches (Atlanta: John Knox Press; Philadelphia: Westminster Press, 1983-85).

to the Scripture that the Bible is canon or "measuring rod" of the church and that it speaks to the church an objective Word of God, illumined by the Holy Spirit and brought home to our hearts by the same Spirit. No. For the deconstructionist, the Bible mediates no objective truth, no ultimate Word from God, no final measure of our belief and action. Indeed, there is no Truth as such that may judge or transform our lives. There are only the meanings that we individuals have already fashioned or desired, and that we have then imposed on the Scriptures. And the God whose thoughts are not our thoughts and whose ways are not our ways (Isa. 55:8), and who so much wants to give us life, remains unknown to all of us who cling to our deadly belief in our own autonomy.

## The Word the Definition of the Church's Life

In this day of secularism and nihilism, the church must therefore reclaim its Scriptures. Or better, the church must let its Scriptures reclaim it, so that the Word of God speaking out of the Scriptures defines and molds and guides the church's whole life. As Karl Barth has written,

> The gospel is not in our thoughts or hearts; it is in scripture. The dearest habits and best insights that I have — I must give them all up before listening. I must not use them to protect myself against the breakthrough of a knowledge that derives from scripture. Again and again I must let myself be contradicted. . . . To let the text straighten out our thinking and not to act as those who are right in the first place — that is what modesty demands.[2]

And certainly that is the disposition that leads one to preach the Word rightly, to let the Word, rather than the preacher's thought, shape the sermon; to proclaim the God-met world of the Bible's view and not the God-deserting world of our contemporary society; to surrender one's own will to the will of the written Word of God and to follow and then proclaim what is said. "Conformity to the Bible is not a quality

2. *Homiletics,* trans. Geoffrey W. Bromiley and Donald E. Daniels (Louisville: Westminster/John Knox Press, 1991), p. 78.

that one can 'choose'," wrote Barth. "It can be understood only as a discipline under which we are simply placed."[3]

The first act in that discipline is to *read* and study and meditate on the Bible. The principal reason the church has lost its Scriptures is because it does not read them and think about them, systematically, day after day. It reads the Bible in bits and pieces, as Sunday morning worship or occasional Bible study demands. It does not read the Scriptures, as a daily habit, from beginning to end, over and over again. But by the power of the Holy Spirit, the Scriptures will speak the Word of God if we will just read and meditate upon them.

To preach and hear the Word rightly, the church must read the whole Bible, however. We cannot fully know either Jesus Christ or who we are as the people of God apart from the Old Testament, and to neglect the Old while focusing exclusively on the New Testament is to leave out two-thirds of the gospel.[4]

Equally important, the church must read the Word of God as a Word spoken into actual history. The Bible is the confession of thousands of people about what God has said and done in their lives and times, and that action of God in time and space is the basis of the Christian faith.

Further, the Word of God incarnate in Christ must not be separated from that history. Christ is not an idea, a metaphor, or a principle of "compassion" or some other virtue, as some contemporary theologians and thinkers would like to make him. As Carl Braaten has written, "The current pluralistic theory of religions, which enjoys a high popularity in some academic circles, advocates that the incarnational dogma and its exclusive claim be deconstructed to myth, fiction, pretense, illusion, opium, crutch, escape, or all of the above."[5] But Christ is none of those things. He is a flesh and blood descendent of Abraham and David, tied irrevocably to their history, and he is the Head of a church that continues in time to this present day. Only in the context of the biblical history can our Lord be rightly understood and preached.

3. Ibid., p. 79.

4. See Elizabeth Achtemeier, *Preaching from the Old Testament* (Louisville: Westminster/John Knox Press, 1989).

5. *No Other Gospel: Christianity Among the World's Religions* (Minneapolis: Fortress Press, 1992), p. 95.

Finally, to preach and hear the Word rightly we must expect God to speak through it. As Karl Barth observes, "The fact of the canon tells us simply that the church has regarded these scriptures as the place where we can expect to hear the voice of God. The proper attitude of preachers does not depend on whether they hold on to the doctrine of inspiration but on whether or not they expect God to speak to them here."[6]

Thus, in approaching the Scriptures to search out what they have to say about abortion, and therefore what we can say and preach about the subject, we here leave behind all of the usual arguments and slogans of our society that have to do with abortion — every claim to "rights" for mother or child, every judgment about "quality of life," every demand that individuals be honored as moral agents, every position framed by court or culture — and we start at the beginning to listen to what God has to say through his Word.

## God the Creator of All Life

Worthy art thou, our Lord and God,
    to receive glory and honor and power,
for thou didst create all things,
    and by thy will they existed and were created.

(Rev. 4:11)

Throughout their pages, the Scriptures affirm that we human beings and all life and all things were created by God, and that fact is basic to preaching about abortion. The universe, indeed the universes (as we would say), with their skies, lands and seas, came into existence and remain in existence only because God said and continues to say, "Let them be!"

Thou art the Lord, thou alone; thou hast made heaven, the heaven of heavens, with all their host, the earth and all that is on it, the seas and all that is in them; and thou preservest all of them; and the host of heaven worships thee. (Neh. 9:6)

6. Barth, *Homiletics*, p. 78.

Because God the Father and God the Son and God the Holy Spirit are one within the Trinity, however, and because God the Son is the Word of God incarnate, Jesus Christ is, in the New Testament, that Word of Genesis 1, through whom God created all things.

> In the beginning was the Word, and the Word was with God, and the Word was God. He was in the beginning with God; all things were made through him, and without him was not anything made that was made. (John 1:1-2)

To God in Jesus Christ we owe our life on this earth. And so the ancient prayer can say, "We bless Thee for our creation, preservation, and all the blessings of this life," just as the Psalmist can praise, "It is he that hath made us and not we ourselves" (Ps. 100:3 KJV). Our life is given us by God in Christ. We are not self-made individuals, nor are we the chance products of nature or the results of indifferent evolution. No. We are the work of his hands (Gen. 2:7, 22; Job 14:15; Ps. 138:8; 119:73), and apart from God in Christ, we would not be. Therefore, all preaching about abortion has first to start with God.

Further, the Scriptures are equally clear that God's work in creating us began while we were still in the wombs of our mothers. "Thou didst form my inward parts," prays the Psalmist, "thou didst knit me together in my mother's womb" (Ps. 139:13). God knew the unborn child he was making, even before it had form (vv. 15-16). So that tiny fertilized egg in your mother that was to become your being was envisioned in its nine-month completion of growth by the Maker who was responsible for your creation. And all along the way, in that gestation period, God worked to shape your substance. Job portrays God's action in marvelous poetry:

> Didst thou not pour me out like milk and curdle me like cheese?
> Thou didst clothe me with skin and flesh,
> > and knit me together with bones and sinews.
>
> > > (Job 10:10)

You were *person* in God's eyes long before you were identifiable in human eyes as belonging to the human race. You were not just "potential person," as some persons who favor abortion have argued, and you certainly were not fowl, fish, beast, insect, or inanimate thing. You were God's human being. And so too is any conceived child, at whatever stage of development in his or her mother's womb. We are not dealing with inanimate blobs of flesh when we speak of abortion; we are dealing with human beings who have been created by God, and who are human beings in his eyes, long before they may look human to us. Consider the human characteristics attributed to the unborn child in Luke 1:15, 41, 44. (See also the appendix, below, on the biological development of the unborn child, by Thomas A. Miller, M.D.)

Again, sermons dealing with abortion often raise the question of when "ensoulment" takes place in an unborn child. But the Scriptures never divide the human person into separate parts of body and soul, despite the fact that English translations of the Scriptures sometimes convey such erroneous conceptions and despite the fact that the church, heavily influenced by ancient Greek thought, has long held to this dualism. The Hebrew word *nephesh*, which is often translated into English as "soul," usually has the meaning of a person's total being or life (cf. Ps. 24:4; 103:1, etc.). To be a living human being, according to the Bible, is to be a psycho-physical whole. Contrary to ancient Greek thought, a person's soul does not exist apart from that person's body: hence, the Christian faith speaks of the resurrection of the body, not of the immortality of the soul. Body and soul cannot be separated, and to be alive in the mother's womb is to be both body and soul from the beginning. The soul is not breathed into the child at some later stage in the child's development.[7]

## God the Owner of All Life

Because God is the Creator of all human life, the Scriptures also affirm that all life belongs to him, and the Christian can never say with those

---

7. According to N. W. Porteous, "Hebrew thought could distinguish soul from body as the material basis of life, but there was no question of two, separate, independent entities. . . . The Hebrew could not conceive of a disembodied *nephesh*." *Interpreter's Dictionary of the Bible* (New York and Nashville: Abingdon, 1962), 4.428. See his entire article on "Soul." See also Robert Jewett, *IDB Supplementary Volume* (New York and Nashville: Abingdon, 1976), pp. 561-562: "The Old Testament legacy is generally carried over into the New Testament in that man is viewed as a totality, with terms such as heart, soul, flesh, or spirit, denoting not a portion but the entire person from a particular point of view."

who support abortion, "My body is my own." "All these things my hand has made," God declares in Isaiah, "and so all these things are mine" (Isa. 66:2).

> For every beast of the forest is mine,
>     the cattle on a thousand hills.
> I know all the birds of the air,
>     and all that moves in the field is mine.
>
> (Ps. 50:10-11)

And so too do we each belong to the One who has made us — we, "the people of his pasture and the sheep of his hand" (Ps. 95:7). He who has made is also he who owns. And so "the earth is the Lord's and the fulness thereof, the world and those who dwell therein" (Ps. 24:1; 1 Cor. 10:26; cf. Deut. 10:14). And God is praised as the Lord and Possessor of all that he has created:

> Thine, O Lord, is the greatness, and the power, and the glory, and the victory, and the majesty; for all that is in the heavens and in the earth is thine; thine is the kingdom, O Lord, and thou art exalted as head above all. (1 Chron. 29:11)

In the Bible's world-view, our children do not belong to us. Christian parents, entrusted with the precious gift of children, know that their offspring are not theirs to do with as they like. Rather, they know that those children belong finally to their heavenly Father, to be lifted up daily before him in prayer, and to be raised in the "nurture and admonition of the Lord" (Eph. 6:4 KJV).

It follows, therefore, that to abort any child in the womb is to destroy a child who belongs finally to God. Indeed, abortion is robbery of God's possession. Malachi 3:8-10 accuses the Israelites of robbing God by not bringing the tithes and offerings of their agricultural products to the temple. How much more, then, are abortions the robbery of those human lives that belong to God! And how much more sternly will such robbery be judged by the Lord!

## God the Lord of All Life

God alone is the Lord of life and death, according to the Scriptures. He alone can "kill and make alive" (Deut. 32:39; cf. 1 Sam. 2:6). He alone can decree capital punishment for murder (Gen. 9:6) or command, "You shall not kill" (Exod. 20:13; Deut. 5:17; Matt. 5:21-22). He alone can give the breath of life (Gen. 2:7) and take it away (Ps. 104:29-30; cf. Ps. 146:4; Eccles. 12:7).

> If he should take back his spirit to himself,
>> and gather to himself his breath,
> all flesh would perish together,
>> and all mortals return to dust.
>
> (Job 34:14-15 NRSV)

For human beings to claim that right over life and death for themselves, whether in abortion or euthanasia, whether dealing with assisted suicide or the denial of medical care to the elderly, is to try to usurp the throne of God and to overstep the bounds of our humanity. We human beings are the creatures of God and not our own Creator, and we cannot in our pride claim to be the lords of life and death.

To be sure, civil government was established by God to protect the innocent and execute judgment against offenders, and it sometimes carries out its duty by means of capital punishment or war. But our creeds constantly warn us to "save the lives of the innocent," because it is sin "to let innocent blood be shed if we can prevent it" (*Scots Confession*, 3.14). *The Larger Westminster Catechism*, speaking of the requirements of God's law, says that it is our duty to avoid all occasions "which tend to the unjust taking away the life of any," and to protect and defend the innocent (7.245).

Our children are given us, despite our sinfulness, only by the grace of God. And we are called to protect and nurture them, from the time of their conception on, as merciful gifts lent to us by a God who is their Creator, Owner, and Lord.

28

# Creation Not Necessary

The wondrous fact about our conception and that of our children is that God did not *have* to make any of us. In our pride, we sometimes are tempted to believe that God cannot get along without us. Thus, the play *Green Pastures,* while marvelously imaginative, gives an erroneous view of God when it portrays the Lord saying to himself, "I'm lonely. I'll make me a world."[8] The truth is that God is not at all lonely, because he is Holy Trinity, within which are enjoyed the love and fellowship of the Father, Son, and Holy Spirit. God alone is the all-sufficient one, needing nothing added to himself.

> The God who made the world and everything in it, he who is Lord of heaven and earth, does not live in shrines made by human hands, nor is he served by human hands, *as though he needed anything,* since he himself gives to all mortals life and breath and all things. (Acts 17:24-25 NRSV)

In short, human life, like the world and all that is in it, is a gift of God, unneeded by the Lord, undeserved by us, and simply given out of God's free-flowing grace. What a miracle it is that God lets us live still one more day! To wake each morning and be alive — that is undeserved gift!

Does not that gift then teach us something about the proper attitude toward the gift of a child in the womb? How many pregnant women have not felt in wonder the first flutterings of life, moving inside of them? How many couples have not gazed with astonishment at the picture of their sixteen-week-old unborn on the ultrasound screen? Or how many new mothers have not lain in their hospital beds, simply overcome with the mystery and awe of it all, unable to speak, as they think about the child they have borne a few hours earlier? Even an unwanted birth, in difficult circumstances, is often touched with the wonder. The fact that God creates and then grows a child in the womb is surely one of the greatest and most miraculous gifts of the Lord in a world filled with wonders.

8. James Weldon Johnson, *God's Trombones: Seven Negro Sermons in Verse* (1927; reprint edn., New York: Viking Press, 1963), p. 17.

If we stand in awe before the gift of God, it is almost inconceivable that we will want to destroy the gift by sucking or scraping it out of the womb. One new father, who saw his son for the first time on the ultrasound screen, declared that from that moment on he could not possibly condone abortion. The son was moving, kicking his legs, waving his arms, floating in the safe waters of his mother, and the father knew that he could only protect that wondrous, living gift. And so he prayed a prayer handed down to him in the tradition of the church:

> O Lord God, in whose hands are the issues of life, we thank Thee for Thy gift to us at this time. We thank Thee for the life given, and the life preserved. And as Thou hast knit together life and love in one fellowship, so we pray Thee to grant that with this fresh gift of life to us, there may be given an increase of love one to another. Grant that the presence of weakness may awaken our tenderness, enable us to minister to the little one that has been given to us in all love, wisdom, and fidelity; and grant that he may live as Thy child, and may serve this generation according to Thy will; through Jesus Christ our Lord. Amen.[9]

## The Purpose of Human Life

This awe and gratitude before the gift of life in the womb raises the question of its purpose. If God did not *have* to make you and me, or the child carried in the womb, then why did he do so? What purpose does God have in mind for any child conceived and formed?

The Scriptures give multiple answers to those questions, which we might sum up in the first answer of the *Shorter Catechism*, which was written by the Westminster Assembly in England in the mid-seventeenth century and which is still used today in Reformed churches. "What is the chief end of man?" asks that document, and the answer follows: "Man's chief end is to glorify God, and to enjoy him forever."

If we divide that answer into its constituent parts, it is clear, first of all, that God creates human beings in order that they may have fellowship with him. Despite the fact that God does not need us and

---

9. Bishop William Boyd Carpenter, 1841. Cited in *A Chain of Prayer Across the Ages* (New York: Dutton and Co. Inc. [New American Edition], 1943), p. 262.

that we add nothing to him, he nevertheless creates us to "enjoy him," to have a relationship with him in which we simply relish being in his company — not because of what he does for us and not because of what he gives to us, but simply because he is the God who he is. We enjoy our friends' company, not for what we can get out of them, but simply for who they are. And so too we are to enjoy God's company simply for who he is. Ours is an enjoyable God! He is much else, but he is surely enjoyable.

Wrote a native convert in India to Charles Haddon Spurgeon in a private letter:

> How I long for my bed! Not that I may sleep — I lie awake often and long! — but to hold sweet communion with my God. . . . The holy joys [the religion propagated by the fisherman of Galilee] brings to me must be from heaven. Do I write this boastingly, brother? Nay, it is with tears of humble gratitude that I tell of the goodness of the Lord.[10]

The Psalmists earlier experienced the same joy in the goodness of God's presence with them.

> Happy are those whom you choose and bring near
>     to live in your courts.
> We shall be satisfied with the goodness of your house,
>     your holy temple.
>
> (Ps. 65:4 NRSV)

> Whom have I in heaven but thee?
>     And there is nothing upon earth that I desire besides thee. . . .
> . . . for me it is good to be near God.
>
> (Ps. 73:25, 28a)

That God allows us into his holy company to enjoy the goodness of his presence is, of course, sheer grace. But he has enlarged the circle of the loving family of the Trinity to include us by adoption and even to allow us to call him "Father" (Matt. 6:9; Rom. 8:15; Gal. 4:6). And one purpose of our life is to enjoy his household and company!

---

10. In C. H. Spurgeon, *Feathers for Arrows* (New York, Chicago: Fleming H. Revell Co., 1875), pp. 173-4.

Abortion, however, denies that purpose for the child in the womb. It denies that God wants that child to be born and to join his household by faith and to call him "Father." It prohibits that child from ever reveling in the joy of an earthly life that is lived in the company of the Father. Indeed, it testifies that God has no interest in that child whatsoever.

The summary statement of the *Shorter Catechism* also says that the purpose for our living is "to glorify God." In the Bible's view that means we are to render God honor, to make him esteemed by all peoples, so that they too know who God is and give praise to him.

> Ascribe to the Lord, O families of the peoples,
> ascribe to the Lord glory and strength!
> Ascribe to the Lord the glory due his name;
> bring an offering, and come into his courts!
> Worship the Lord in holy array;
> tremble before him, all the earth!
>
> (Ps. 96:7-9)

We honor the Lord by acknowledging that he is Lord of our lives, that his is the will to be done on earth even as it is in heaven, and that therefore we are to obey his will and serve his purpose. Anything less than that is a denial of his lordship and therefore a besmirching of his name and honor. It is, as in the Decalogue, a taking of the Lord's name in vain (Exod. 20:7), an attempt to make him less than the Lord he is.

But abortion not only denies to the unborn child that opportunity to honor and serve his or her Lord. It also denies that God knew what he was doing when he created the child in the womb in the first place. Abortion sets above the will of God the will of sinful human beings who, in place of the life that God has decreed, choose death instead.

We also glorify God when we praise his holy name, when we recount to other persons what God has done throughout his holy history and what he has done in our church or in our personal lives. "It is good to sing praises to our God," exclaims the Psalmist, "for he is gracious, and a song of praise is seemly" (Ps. 147:1). In the Great Thanksgiving of the Communion Service, the church "with Angels and Archangels, and with all the company of heaven" lauds and magnifies God's holy Name, evermore praising him "and saying, Holy, holy, holy,

32

Lord God of Hosts: Heaven and earth are full of thy glory. Glory be to thee, O Lord Most High."[11]

"Let everything that breathes praise the Lord," reads the last verse in the Psalter. Indeed, in the Bible's view, such praise is synonymous with life, for "The dead do not praise the Lord, nor do any that go down in silence" (Ps. 115:17), and not to praise the Lord is therefore to be as good as dead. One of the purposes of our living, says the catechism, is to raise our voices to God in thankful, joyful praise.

If a child is killed in the womb, however, and aborted, that child will never raise his or her voice in such praise. God will listen for his child and will hear only silence. And God's purpose for that child's life will have been thwarted. Charles Wesley wrote in his famous hymn, "O for a thousand tongues to sing my dear Redeemer's praise." Abortion every year reduces the number, not by a thousand, but by one and one-half million.

In short, abortion denies all these purposes for human life. It denies that a child in the womb has a purpose planned for him or her by God: that God wants that child to join his earthly family and enjoy his company; that God wills for that child to serve his lordly will and so honor his name; that God desires to hear that child's voice raised to him in loving praise.

The chief end of humankind is to glorify the Lord and enjoy him forever. And every child is made for that purpose. Indeed, even the child ill-conceived through rape or incest, even the child deformed in the womb, can enter into and participate in these God-given purposes for human life. (See Chapter 6 for a fuller discussion.) But abortion is a denial of God's purpose and therefore finally a denial of God and of his lordship. Abortion is human will set above God's, and therefore finally nihilism — death.[12]

---

11. *The Book of Common Prayer.*

12. In debates about abortion, the question often arises as to how we are to view spontaneous abortions. According to the *New England Journal of Medicine* 319.4 (July 28, 1944), some 31 to 52 percent of human conceptions end in miscarriages. If God is the Creator and Owner of all human life, did he not care for such children and have a purpose for them? We were asked that poignant question by an acquaintance who desperately wanted to have children, and yet who was unable to carry to term any one of her three unborn.

Certainly there are mysteries surrounding the sufferings known in human

If the church is rightly to preach and to hear the Word of God and thus demonstrate the characteristic marks of the church, then surely when the church is speaking about the crucial issue of abortion in our time, these views from the Scriptures must inform the message.

---

life that defy all explanation. But it can also be said that the sinfulness of the human race as a whole — not necessarily of the individual woman, but of the race as a whole — has corrupted even our genes, our procreation, and our sexuality, so that what God would give in his love is prevented from coming to fruition. God gives the wondrous gift of conception, only to have his intention thwarted by the fallen condition of us all. As Paul writes, "the whole creation has been groaning in travail together until now; and not only the creation, but we ourselves" (Rom. 8:22-23). And that fallenness, which brings with it suffering and sorrow, evil and death, will not be fully overcome until God brings in his kingdom in its fullness, and death and mourning, crying and pain will have passed away (Rev. 21:4).

# CHAPTER 3

# *Baptism Rightly Administered*

On a late autumn afternoon some time ago, a friend of ours happened to drive by the local abortion clinic. There were not many cars parked in front of the clinic at that hour, nor were there women going in and out. But there was a grey van at the curb, with black lettering on its side. And the lettering read, "Medical Wastes."

That is the sign of abortion: "Medical Wastes" — hundreds of unborn children forcefully removed from the wombs of their mothers and consigned to garbage bags, to be hauled off to the incinerator.

That is a sign that the church needs to think about, for the church has a sign that directly contradicts the sign of abortion. The church has the sign of baptism. Baptism is the sign and seal of our incorporation into the church, the Body of Christ. It is the outward, visible action by which we are initiated into the new life that is to characterize the Christian community of the church. And in all of its meanings, baptism stands opposed to abortion. In order to understand that, however, we must understand the meaning of a sacrament and then, in particular, the meaning of baptism.

## What Is a Sacrament?

Ever since its beginning, the church throughout the world has celebrated at least two sacraments, baptism and the Lord's Supper, as the two rites which, according to the New Testament, were commanded

35

for his church by Christ (Matt. 28:18-20; 1 Cor. 11:23-25; cf. Mark 14:22-25 and parallels). Along with the Word rightly preached, the proper celebration of these two sacraments is an essential mark of the church. Where the Word is rightly preached and the sacraments are rightly administered, there is the true church of Christ.

In understanding the meaning of a sacrament, it is important to distinguish it from a sacrifice. The latter is what the church renders to God — its sacrifice of praise and thanksgiving, for example. But a sacrament is what God gives to the church. A sacrament is God's self-giving, God pouring out his life upon his people, God acting in their lives or, as Augustine defined it, "the visible form of an invisible grace."

We take the name "sacrament" from the Latin word *sacramentum*, which is the way a second century church Father, Tertullian, translated the Greek word, *mysterion*, "mystery." A *sacramentum*, in its original usage, was the oath taken by Roman soldiers, but as H. S. Coffin has observed,

> Sacraments are not pledges which Christians make to God; but pledges which he makes to us, and pledges which actually convey to us that which is pledged when we receive it in faith. In the Sacraments God is himself both the Giver and the Gift. They are his actions and belong in common worship.[1]

The fact that it is God and not human beings who act in a sacrament is illustrated by some churches' practice of infant baptism. The infant is brought before the congregation by the faith of the parents, but the infant does nothing to make the baptism effective. Rather, the infant receives God's action through the sacrament. God gives the gift. The gift is then nurtured by the parents' instruction of the child and by the child's later confirmation and growth in the faith. But initially, the action in baptism is God's and God's alone. God's grace is always "prevenient," that is, it always precedes the human response to it.

Further, a sacrament makes visible, by use of an object (water, bread, wine) and an action, that which has been spoken in the Word. For example, the Word announces that Christ died for our sins, and the Lord's Supper then offers to us the broken bread: "This is my body

---

1. Henry Sloane Coffin, *The Public Worship of God* (Philadelphia: Westminster Press, 1946), p. 136.

which is broken for you." So Word and sacrament belong together and reinforce one another. As a kiss reinforces the words "I love you," so the action of the sacrament reinforces the proclamation of the Word. And as the words "I love you" interpret the kiss, so the Word interprets the action of the sacrament. A sacrament is not just a remembering of God's act in Christ in the past. It is that action made present in the life of the worshiping congregation. Word and sacrament belong together and constitute the essential marks of the church.

## Baptism and Death's Defeat

The Scriptures tell us that baptism is our participation in the death and resurrection of Jesus Christ (Rom. 6:3-11; Col. 2:12), and because it seals our victory over death, it is a direct contradiction of abortion.

Our Lord was put to death on the cross of Calvary by the sins of humanity (Rom. 5:8). Indeed, the best that human beings could muster — the best Roman law, the best Jewish faith, along with our best but always selfish aspirations, actions, and piety — nailed Jesus to the tree. The Negro spiritual asks, "Were you there when they crucified my Lord?" and the answer is, "We were." We crucified him.

> What Thou, my Lord, has suffered
>> Was all for sinners' gain:
> Mine, mine was the transgression,
>> But Thine the deadly pain.
> Lo, here I fall, my Savior!
>> 'Tis I deserve Thy place;
> Look on me with Thy favor,
>> Vouchsafe to me Thy grace.[2]

"The wages of sin is death," writes Paul (Rom. 6:23), and Christ took all of our sins upon himself and died the death we deserved at the hands of God.

But Christ was raised from the dead on the first day of the week,

---

2. "O Sacred Head, Now Wounded," second stanza. This 12th century Latin hymn was first translated by Paul Gerhardt in 1656; the English translation cited here is by James W. Alexander, 1830.

thereby overcoming the power of the sin that crucified him and breaking the bonds of death that held him captive. "For we know that Christ being raised from the dead will never die again; death no longer has dominion over him" (Rom. 6:9). And we, say the Scriptures, are baptized into that victory. "You were buried with him in baptism, in which you were also raised with him through faith in the working of God, who raised him from the dead" (Col. 2:12). God, in our baptism, decreed life for us and not death. " 'Death is swallowed up in victory. O death, where is thy victory? O death, where is thy sting?' " (1 Cor. 15:54-55).

Abortion, however, is death. The final destination of the aborted child is the medical waste truck and the fire of the incinerator. And that is a ghastly contradiction of what the church says in its baptismal rite. The church proclaims by its sacrament the defeat of death. But abortion proclaims the victory of death over the life God has given. If the church endorses abortion, it contradicts everything it confesses in its initiatory rite.

## Adoption by Baptism

The Scriptures also tell us that when we were baptized, we were adopted by God as his children (Gal. 3:26–4:7); therefore we can no longer countenance the abortionist claim that we belong to ourselves alone.

When we decided that we could live without our heavenly Father and manage our own lives, we estranged ourselves from the household of God, much like that Prodigal Son in Luke 15:11-24, who went into a "far country" and ended up feeding swine. Apart from God, we stumbled into wrong and hungered for *something* and felt lost and alone.

But in baptism the Father joyfully (cf. Luke 15:7) forgave us our estrangement from him, as much as to say, "This my [child] was dead, and is alive again; [this child] was lost, and is found" (Luke 15:24). God took us back into his household, as beloved family members, and made us heirs, through his adoption of us, of all he has promised (Gal. 3:29; 4:7; Rom. 8:17).

The water of baptism symbolizes that forgiveness and adoption,

38

for it is the sign that we are washed clean once again, not by the actual water but by the Holy Spirit given with it (Acts 2:38; 22:16; Heb. 10:22; 1 Pet. 3:21). Thus, the church prays before the baptismal action:

> Set apart this water from a common to a sacred use, and grant that what we now do on earth may be confirmed in heaven. As in humble faith we present (Name) to Thee, we beseech Thee to receive him/her, to endue him/her with Thy Holy Spirit, and to keep him/her ever as Thine own; through Jesus Christ our Lord. Amen. (*The Book of Common Worship*, 1946)

Having been given the Spirit according to the promise of God, the baptized can then call God "Father" (Rom. 8:15; Gal. 4:6) and take his or her place in the family of God, as the Father's beloved child.

In short, the one who is baptized no longer belongs to the world, or to the enslaving spectres of sin and death. No. The one who is baptized belongs to God, and is a member of his family, his child. And the Scriptures further tell us that nothing in all creation, then, "neither death nor life, nor angels, nor principalities, nor things present, nor things to come, nor powers" (Rom. 8:38-39) of this world or of another, can wrest the baptized person out of the hand of the God who loves him or her in Jesus Christ. Contrary to the abortionist's claim of autonomy, the baptized person belongs to God and to nothing and no one else, not even to him or herself.

Paul emphasizes that belonging when he writes, "You are not your own; you were bought with a price" (1 Cor. 6:19-20; cf. 7:23) — namely, the redemption price of the death of Christ on the cross, for "to redeem" in biblical usage means to buy back a family member who has fallen into slavery (cf. Lev. 25:47-55). In baptism, God claims us as his *family member* and buys us back from our slavery to sin and death.

So too, Christ's command that we be baptized "in the name of the Father and of the Son and of the Holy Spirit" (Matt. 28:19) emphasizes that we belong to God. We take on the family name of the Triune God.

> By baptizing in the name of the Father, the Apostles made it clear that those baptized have been adopted as children of the Father. By baptizing in the name of the Son, the Apostles made it clear that those baptized were to be joined to Christ in his death and resur-

rection. By baptizing in the name of the Holy Spirit, they made it clear that baptism in water is a prophetic sign of being baptized in the Holy Spirit.[3]

It is no wonder that Martin Luther, in times of doubt and distress, found his greatest comfort by reminding himself, "I am baptized," for the baptized person is God's. The infant who is brought by his or her parents to the baptismal font can no longer be claimed eternally by the powers of evil and death, just as no baptized adult can be claimed eternally by those powers. For the baptized person has been claimed by God as his own, and God will not surrender him or her.

Abortion, however, denies these claims that the church makes about baptism. Advocates of abortion loudly tell us that they belong to themselves alone. "My body is my own," runs the slogan. But further, advocates of abortion make the claim that the child in the womb belongs to the woman who carries it, that the mother is therefore free to do away with that child if she wishes.

The church that baptizes, however, wants us all to belong to God. And the promise that we can become children of God (cf. John 1:12-13) is given not only to us, but to all of our children and future children. "The promise is to you and to your children and to all that are far off, every one whom the Lord our God calls to him" (Acts 2:39; cf. Deut. 29:14). How, then, can the Christian Church possibly endorse the self-justifying claim of the advocates of abortion that we will always belong only to ourselves? How can we endorse such a claim when it gives the lie to one of our central beliefs about baptism?

## Baptism and the Future

The Scriptures also tell us that baptism marks our entrance into the new age of the kingdom of God. As Karl Barth has written, "Life begins with baptism, not with birth."[4] Or as the New Testament puts it, we have been "born anew" (1 Pet. 1:3, 23). We are born anew for a future, but of course abortion cuts off all possibility of a child's future.

3. Hughes Oliphant Old, *Worship* (Atlanta: John Knox Press, 1984), p. 11.
4. *Homiletics*, p. 58.

As we were created by God in the beginning, and yet were then corrupted by sin, so we are re-created by God in Christ in baptism, through the work of the Holy Spirit (John 3:1-8). We are made new creatures in Jesus Christ, new creations, with new beginnings and new possibilities. "The old has passed away, behold, the new has come" (2 Cor. 5:17). We now are not only recipients, through the action of the Holy Spirit, of the forgiveness of God in Christ; we now are partakers of the powers of that new age of the kingdom inaugurated in the person of Christ (cf. Mark 1:15; Luke 11:20; 17:21; Matt. 3:2). We are no longer enslaved to the powers of the world and of sin; we now can do the good and live lives of righteousness (Rom. 6:15-19). For as Paul says, the fruits of the Spirit given us in our baptism are "love, joy, peace, patience, kindness, goodness, faithfulness, gentleness, self-control." The baptized person can be a transformed person, growing in what the church calls "sanctification," growing in grace (cf. Phil. 1:9-11), until we all attain "to maturity, to the measure of the full stature of Christ" (Eph. 4:13 NRSV).

In other words, because of our baptism, we have a future and a hope. The Holy Spirit has been given us in order that, over the years, we may live out our baptism, growing more and more into the likeness of Christ. Indeed, says Paul, this is the work of the Spirit in us, that he continues to change us into the likeness of Christ, "from one degree of glory to another" (2 Cor. 3:18). By the work of the Holy Spirit, we can become Christ-like persons.

What is more, we enter into a holy history that God is working out in his world. We become part of God's story that he is creating, the story that will finally end with the kingdom of God coming on earth even as it is now in heaven. The story began long before we were baptized, and it will continue, if God so wills, long after we have died on earth. But our lives that are hid with God in Christ are given a meaning far beyond our little sphere of time and space, because they participate in God's history that spans all time and space. And they strain forward to that future goal when the "the kingdom of the world" has indeed become "the kingdom of our Lord and of his Christ" (Rev. 11:15).

The church knows there is a future, a future that will be created and governed by God. But for the aborted child, there is no future. There are only a few brief weeks in the haven of the womb and then extinction.

The abortion advocate argues in reply that many children, if allowed to be born, would have no "future" deserving of the term. Rather their life would be one of lovelessness and misery and suffering, ending in crime and poverty. But as theologian Ray Anderson has written in another connection, we have no right to disqualify anyone simply because we think we know his or her destiny here on earth.[5] Do we ever really know what purpose and future God has planned for any particular individual?

In its October 21, 1992, issue, the *Christian Century* published a moving article entitled "Baptism in a Coffin," by Ralph C. Wood. It concerned the conversion and subsequent baptism of a man imprisoned for the terrible crime of molesting his ten-year-old daughter. The man's conversion was not an insincere attempt to gain early parole, however, but was prompted by the forgiveness given him by his wife and daughter — once again the work of God's prevenient grace.

> It was only then — when freed from the burden of his sin by God's humanly mediated grace — that the molester got on his knees and begged for the mercy of both God and his family.[6]

As a result, the prison chaplain agreed to baptize him into the Christian faith.

The only baptismal "font" available was a plastic-lined wooden coffin, and so the prisoner, burdened with his despicable crime, was lowered by the chaplain into the death of Christ and raised from the waters, washed clean of his past and given a future by the resurrection of Christ. "I'm now a free man," he declared, refusing to change his dripping clothes. "I'm not impatient to leave prison because this wire can't shackle my soul. I know that I deserved to come here, to pay for what I did. But I also learned here that Someone else has paid for all my crimes: my sins against God."[7] And his final resolution was to return to his hometown, despite his former shame, to resume his work as a carpenter, and to become a faithful father and husband. "More important by far, he declared his hope to join a local church and to

---

5. *The Gospel According to Judas* (Colorado Springs: Helmers and Howard, 1991), p. 51.

6. P. 926.

7. Ibid.

live out his new life in Christ as a public witness to the transforming power of God's grace."[8]

All of this took place, despite the fact that many "friends" had counseled the mother and daughter never to forgive or accept the man again: we human beings make the mistake of believing that we know exactly what someone's future will be. We even sometimes think we know what the future will be for an unborn child. But as Ray Anderson writes, "What really counts is what we receive from the hand of God."[9] No person's destiny is an irrevocable fate, because God is always at work. Indeed, no child's future need be judged so black that it would be better for the child not to be born, because God, present through the Spirit of Christ, is always at work in a faithful church, and the church, if it will, can change the future of any child who seems destined only for suffering.

The advocates of abortion deny those facts, of course. They deny that God can work in any life, and they deny that the church can be the instrument of God to bring good to a child seemingly destined only for evil. Abortion is resignation, throwing up one's hands and deciding that nothing can be changed, and especially not the future. But God in Jesus Christ can make all things new and give a future and a hope where none seem possible. And the Christian Church is called to proclaim and act upon that joyful good news.

## Baptism into the New Community

The Scriptures further tell us that baptism is never simply a private act, as if its goal were to "save" an individual and assure his or her eventual entrance into heaven. Baptisms are not private ceremonies and should not be conducted as such. Rather, baptism is the initial rite by which we become members of the Body of Christ, the church universal, and so it lays upon the church the responsibility for welcoming, rather than aborting, its children.

> For by one Spirit we were all baptized into one body — Jews or Greeks, slaves or free — and all were made to drink of one Spirit.

8. Ibid.
9. *Gospel According to Judas*, p. 79.

For the body does not consist of one member but of many. (1 Cor. 12:13-14)

God's activity in his world, according to the Bible, has as one of its primary goals the creation of a new people, of a community, of a church if you will, that knows how to live in love and righteousness and peace under his guiding lordship. In the Old Testament, that people was Israel; in the New, it is the Christian Church, that can encompass not only the Israel of old, but the entire world of nations, Jew and Greek, slave and free, male and female, who are all to become one in Christ Jesus (Gal. 3:27-28).

Biblically speaking, we can never be Christians all by ourselves, for we are bidden not only to love our God, but also to love our neighbor (Mark 12:30-31), and that immediately involves us in community in the most intimate and concrete way. It is easy to say we love all people, but when we are commanded to love our neighbor, we have to deal with particular individuals whom we may not even like very well. "Bear one another's burdens," writes Paul, "and so fulfill the law of Christ" (Gal. 6:2). "As we have opportunity, let us do good to all . . . and especially to those who are of the household of faith" (v. 10).

Into the new community of the church, God wishes to draw all people, until finally every knee has bowed and every tongue confessed that "Jesus Christ is Lord, to the glory of God the Father" (Phil. 2:10-11; cf. Isa. 45:22-23) — until finally God has become all in all to every nation and person, and all things in heaven and on earth have been united in Christ (Eph. 1:10), in that realm called the kingdom of God.

Baptism is the rite of passage by which each individual enters into the church, the new universal community that God is forming on earth. In baptism, the new member is united with every other member of the community, because the Body of Christ the church is one, and all are made one in him. Baptism into church membership anticipates that final unity of all things in Christ, envisioned in Ephesians 1:10; it is a foretaste of the final unity of the kingdom of God.

We are thus responsible for one another in the community of the church — that is the primary message of 1 John. We are to love one another, because Christ has first loved us (1 John 4:19). We inherit that responsibility with the new life given us in our baptism.

We know that we have passed from death to life, because we love one another. Whoever does not love abides in death. (1 John 3:14 NRSV)

Because this is true, we are responsible for every pregnant woman who is baptized into our community. As Stanley Hauerwas and William Willimon have written, "we cannot say to the pregnant fifteen-year old, 'Abortion is a sin. It is your problem.' Rather, it is *our* problem. We ask ourselves what sort of church we would need to be to enable an ordinary person like her to be the sort of disciple Jesus calls her to be."[10] We take upon ourselves the responsibility for nurturing every pregnancy within our fellowship, whether it was planned or unplanned, whether it is welcomed or unwelcomed. Indeed, we reach out to draw all persons into our fellowship, including those who have "problem pregnancies," and we proclaim to them that by baptism into Christ's Body, the church, they are forgiven and adopted by God as his own beloved children, and that they are by baptism now a part of our church family, which will love them and share their problems and help them bring forth their children.

Further, as the Body of Christ, we assure such women that when their children are born, those children will also be welcomed and nurtured in our fellowship. ("The promise is to you and your children," Acts 2:39.) Unfortunately, the church has not always done that.

In many of our modern, sophisticated congregations, children are often viewed as distractions. . . . Adult members sometimes complain that they cannot pay attention to the sermon, they cannot listen to the beautiful music, when fidgety children are beside them in the pews.[11]

Consequently, we have created "children's church" so these distracting children can be removed, in order that we adults can pay attention. But as Hauerwas and Willimon point out, Jesus put a child "in the midst of them" (Matt. 18:1-4) for the precise purpose of helping the disciples pay attention. "The child, in Jesus' mind, was not an annoy-

10. *Resident Aliens* (Nashville: Abingdon Press, 1989), p. 81.
11. Ibid., p. 96.

ing distraction. The child was a last-ditch effort by God to help the disciples pay attention to the odd nature of God's kingdom."[12]

When children are baptized into the church, they become a part of that fellowship which looks forward to the kingdom's unity of all things and persons in Christ. And so the church, in anticipation of that, accepts responsibility for every baptized child, and the charge to the congregation to nurture the child is, in many denominations, a part of the baptismal rite. For example, in the 1946 *Book of Common Worship*, the minister directs these words to the congregation:

> This Child is now received into Christ's Church: And you the people of this congregation in receiving this Child promise with God's help to be his/her sponsor to the end that he/she may confess Christ as his/her Lord and Saviour and come at last to His eternal kingdom. Jesus said, Whoso shall receive one such little child in My name receiveth Me.

In a modern liturgy of the Presbyterian Church (USA) and Cumberland Presbyterian Church, there is a response given by the congregation to the charge from the minister:

> With joy and thanksgiving,
> we welcome you into Christ's church;
> for we are all one in Christ.
> We promise to love, encourage, and support you,
> to share the good news of the gospel with you,
> and to help you know and follow Christ.[13]

In the Methodist Church, the response by the congregation includes the promise to *be the church,* to be the kind of community that will enable the newly baptized to become a faithful disciple of Christ:

> We give thanks for all that God has already given you
> and we welcome you in Christian love.
> As members together with you
> in the body of Christ

12. Ibid.

13. *Holy Baptism and Services for the Renewal of Baptism,* Supplemental Liturgical Resource 12 (Philadelphia: The Westminster Press, 1985).

> and in this congregation
> of the United Methodist Church,
> we renew our covenant
> faithfully to participate
> in the ministries of the church
> by our prayers, our presence,
> our gifts, and our service,
> that in everything God may be glorified
> through Jesus Christ.[14]

All of these words from the baptismal rite are examples of how the church, by rightly administering and living out its sacrament, constitutes itself as the church. "The church must be created new, in each generation, not through procreation but through baptism."[15] And baptism can only be properly celebrated if the church welcomes its born and unborn children and their mothers.

How terrible it is, then, when the church disavows that responsibility for every life within its community — when it counsels *or even aids,* by financial support or transportation, some pregnant woman to abort her child, and refuses to accept and nurture a child whom God has created. "Whoever receives one such child in my name receives me," Jesus taught, "but whoever causes one of these little ones who believe in me to sin, it would be better for him to have a great millstone fastened round his neck and to be drowned in the depth of the sea" (Matt. 18:5-6). Jesus issues that warning as a judgment from the God who has created every child, and it is a warning that needs to be heeded by every church that sanctions abortion and by every religious body that belongs to the Religious Coalition for Reproductive Choice. Our secular and indifferent society pays little heed to statements about the judgment of God, but the New Testament pays great heed: it reminds us that "It is a fearful thing to fall into the hands of the living God" (Heb. 10:31).

If the church will truly be the church, however, and if the church's members will live out their *own* baptismal calling, in the power of the Holy Spirit given them (John 20:21-22), by heeding Christ's commis-

---

14. *The United Methodist Hymnal: Book of United Methodist Worship* (Nashville: The United Methodist Publishing House, 1989), p. 43.

15. *Resident Aliens,* p. 60.

47

sion to make disciples of all people (Matt. 28:19), then the church can truly minister as the Body of Christ to those in need — the unmarried teenager who thinks she has no option but abortion; the poverty-stricken woman with child who already has six children and who thinks she can afford no more; the terrified college student who has conceived as a result of date-rape; the sinful, the victimized, the poor, the fearful, the ashamed.

More than that, if the church will truly be the church by welcoming all children, then it can minister in integrity to those who have tragically and prematurely lost a child. In its 1989 book of worship, for example, the United Methodist Church includes "A Service of Death and Resurrection for a Stillborn Child" and "A Service of Hope After Loss of Pregnancy." One of the prayers in the latter service begins like this:

> Life-giving God,
> your love surrounded each of us in our mothers' wombs,
> and from that secret place you called us forth to life.
> Pour out your compassion upon (Mother's Name).
> Her heart is heavy with the loss of the promise
>     that once took form in her womb. . . .

And a following prayer ends with these words:

> In our pain and confusion we look to you, Lord,
>     in whom no life is without meaning, however small or brief.
> Let not our limited understanding confine our faith.
> Draw us closer to you and closer to each other.
> Lay our broken hearts open in faith to you
>     and in ever greater compassion to one another.
> So raise us from death to life; we pray in Christ's name. Amen.

Only the church that values the life of every child, and that hoped for the deceased child to join its fellowship, can pray those prayers with integrity. The church that thought it better for the child to be aborted can offer little comfort when that violent death is then mourned.

So the church is called rightly to celebrate its rite of baptism: to affirm in word and deed that God has willed life for each of his children; that God wishes to adopt into his loving family every child he has created; that God plans a future for his children and calls his church to welcome and protect and nurture them, that finally they too may enter into abundant life in Christ and look forward to eternal life in the company of their Father.

# CHAPTER 4

# *The Supper Rightly Celebrated*

The celebration of the Lord's Supper has ever been regarded by the Church as the innermost sanctuary of the whole Christian worship. We have to do here not with signs merely, but with the realities which these signs represent. The Lord's Table, therefore, can be rightly approached only by those who are of a devout, repentant, and believing mind. (Evangelical and Reformed *Book of Worship*, 1947)

## The Reaffirmation of Baptism

If everything that we have said about baptism is true, then it is very difficult to see how anything having to do with abortion can be joined together with anything having to do with the Lord's Supper, for the Supper gathers up all the meaning of baptism that we have previously discussed and renews it for members of the Body of Christ. The Supper is the feast that our Lord Jesus Christ has given as a gift to those who belong to him through baptism. It is the glad celebration given to believers, the joyful communion of the church with its sovereign Head.

In this respect, the Lord's Supper is a covenant meal, finally finding its original roots in the covenant "cut" and the meal eaten in God's presence by Moses and the representatives of his people Israel on Mt. Sinai (Exod. 24:3-11). That covenant communion probably was renewed yearly between God and his people, in a covenant renewal cere-

51

mony (cf. Deuteronomy, especially 29:10-15), and so too, the Lord's Supper is the covenant renewal ceremony of the Christian Church.

At the heart of the ceremony in Israel was the promise of God, "I will be their God, and they shall be my people" (Lev. 26:12; Jer. 31:1; Ezek. 37:23, 27; 2 Cor. 6:16; Rev. 21:3; cf. Gen. 17:7-8; Exod. 29:45). And the responding promise of the people was, "All that the Lord has spoken we will do, and we will be obedient" (Exod. 24:7; cf. 19:8). Thus, the covenant implied Israel's obedience to the covenant command, "You shall have no other gods before me" (Exod. 20:3) and to all the commands that followed.

Because Israel repeatedly broke her covenant with the Lord, she was judged for her unfaithfulness and sent into exile. Nevertheless, God in his mercy promised that he would make a new covenant with his elected people:

> The days are surely coming, says the Lord, when I will make a new covenant with the house of Israel and the house of Judah. It will not be like the covenant which I made with their ancestors when I took them by the hand to bring them out of the land of Egypt — a covenant that they broke, though I was their husband, says the Lord. But this is the covenant that I will make with the house of Israel after those days, says the Lord: I will put my law within them, and I will write it on their hearts; and I will be their God, and they shall be my people. No longer shall they teach one another, or say to each other, "Know the Lord," for they shall all know me, from the least of them to the greatest, says the Lord; for I will forgive their iniquity, and remember their sin no more. (Jer. 31:31-34 NRSV; cf. Hos. 2:16-23)

It was that promise of a new covenant between God and his people that our Lord Jesus fulfilled on the night he was betrayed, when he took the cup at the Last Supper with his disciples and gave it to them, saying, "This cup is the *new covenant* in my blood. Do this, as often as you drink it, in remembrance of me" (1 Cor. 11:25).

Thus, those who approach the Lord's table do so with the same promise as that made by ancient Israel: "All that the Lord has spoken we will do, and we will be obedient." In short, those who eat and drink at the Lord's Supper are those who deliberately surrender themselves to the lordship of Jesus Christ. They are those who put themselves under his commandments, who repent of their daily failures to be obedient, and who promise anew to walk in his ways and obey his will as given them through the Scriptures. Such promises are surely relevant to the issue of abortion.

Many churches still have preparatory services in which the people examine their lives and repent and prepare themselves to pledge themselves anew at the Supper to be God's people. But one of the traditional prefaces to the confession of sin before the Supper also encapsulates that preparation:

> Ye who do truly and earnestly repent of your sins, and are in love and charity with your neighbors, and intend to lead a new life, following the commandments of God, and walking from henceforth in his holy ways: Draw near with faith, and take this Holy Sacrament to your comfort; and make your humble confession to Almighty God. (*The Book of Common Worship*, 1946)

The result is that we find within the liturgies of the Lord's Supper all of those elements of the baptized life that we have discussed in the preceding chapter.

For example, in the Great Prayer of Thanksgiving which precedes the distribution of the elements, there is thanks given for God's creation of all the world, and for his creation of us in his image: we belong to the one who has made us, and so we are not free to do with our bodies only what we like. There is a recounting of the holy history ruled by God, which makes it clear that life is governed by his will and not by ours: we are not our own, and so we are responsible to God for our born and unborn children. Then follows that song of praise and benediction by the communion of the faithful in all times and places, which constitutes the purpose of our life and which so contradicts the silence of abortion:

> Therefore with Angels and Archangels, and with all the company of heaven, we laud and magnify thy glorious Name; evermore praising thee, and saying,

> > Holy, holy, holy, Lord God of Hosts:
> > Heaven and earth are full of thy glory.
> > Glory be to thee, O Lord Most High.
> > Blessed is he that cometh in the name of the Lord.
> > Hosanna in the highest.

> > > (*The Book of Common Prayer*, 1977)

After the praise there follows the *anamnesis,* the "remembering" of the incarnation, life, death, resurrection, ascension, and intercession of Christ, and then Jesus' words when he instituted the Supper, all of which acknowledge the fact that when we fell into slavery to sin and death, God bought us back by the death and resurrection of his Son, and made us adopted members of his household, in a community of the faithful, with a future and a hope. All that has been said in relation to baptism is repeatedly reaffirmed by our celebration of the Lord's Supper, and the claims of autonomy and self-determination made by the advocates of abortion crumble before that feast's holy mystery.

## Grace to Tell the Truth

The essential nature of the Supper is the unity of the body. It is through the mystery of the Supper, said John Calvin, that we grow into one body with Christ.[1] But it is a unity respectful of the truth. The Book of Order of the Presbyterian Church notes that a "historic principle of church order" is, namely,

> that truth is in order to goodness; and the great touchstone of truth, its tendency to promote holiness, according to our Savior's rule, "By their fruits ye shall know them." And that no opinion can be either more pernicious or more absurd than that which brings truth and falsehood upon a level, and represents it as of no consequence what a man's opinions are. On the contrary, we are persuaded that there is an inseparable connection between faith and practice, truth and duty. Otherwise, it would be of no consequence either to discover truth or to embrace it.[2]

The church, in its treatment of abortion, must learn and agree to tell the truth.

Unfortunately, however, the church has often sanitized the discussion of abortion and thereby hidden the truth from church members. For example, the ruling officer of one denomination declared

1. *Institutes of the Christian Religion* 4.12.
2. *The Constitution of the Presbyterian Church (U.S.A.),* Part II, Book of Order, Form of Government, I, Preliminary Principles, G-1.0304.

language about "killing" to be "out of bounds" in debate about abortion. He wanted to avoid words that signify that abortion destroys a human life. One pastor, in leading a series on abortion, refused to allow display of anatomically accurate models of the developing unborn child because, she said, they evoked an emotional reaction in the context of a discussion of abortion.

In a similar vein, the church rarely discusses the methods of abortion, preferring not to mention the curettage, suction, and saline methods that are used to kill and dismember the child in the womb. As so often in our culture, language is omitted or softened to shield us from reality and the true nature of our sin.

Nevertheless, participation in the Lord's Supper demands that we tell the truth, that we squarely face and name exactly what we have done and are doing with respect to abortion. And the characteristic of the Lord's Supper that allows us to do that is the forgiveness offered us in the Supper by the atoning death and resurrection of our Lord. As Ray Anderson has written, "Shame is healed not by exposing failure and weakness, but through empowering the self through the gift of grace and love."[3]

That grace and love are the incomparable gifts given us under the signs of the bread and wine: Christ's body broken for even us, Christ's blood shed for even us, fulfilling God's promise in the new covenant, "I will forgive their iniquity, and I will remember their sin no more" (Jer. 31:34). We the waffling church, we the compromising Body of Christ, we the ashamed company of the covenant, who do not want to speak of abortion and its blood and killing, are, at the table of Christ, forgiven for our cowardice and compromise, and enabled to speak the truth about this terrible evil in our society — enabled to speak the horror when no one else will acknowledge it.

It is absolutely necessary that we learn to speak that truth about abortion — and about the sexual practices that often lead to abortion — for only then can the forgiveness and reconciliation and healing offered to us at the Lord's table have any meaning.

> If we say we have no sin, we deceive ourselves, and the truth is not in us. If we confess our sins, he is faithful and just, and will forgive our sins and cleanse us from all unrighteousness. (1 John 1:8-9)

3. *The Gospel According to Judas* (Colorado Springs: Helmers and Howard, 1991), p. 138.

A pastor-friend of ours told the story of a woman who had undergone an abortion, and who came to him for counseling. She was deeply troubled by what she had done, and she had consulted numerous psychologists and therapists in the effort to ease her conscience. When she told the pastor her story, he replied to her, "You have done wrong." Her grateful response was, "That's what I wanted to hear." She wanted *someone* to acknowledge what she knew in her inner self — that she had sinfully killed another human being, because until that was confessed, she could not receive Christ's forgiveness and healing of her past. She could not become the new creature in Christ that her Lord's death and resurrection, remembered at the Supper, offered to her.

If the church will speak truthfully about abortion, there is One who can forgive the sin and heal the pain. And the very grace, offered once and for all on Calvary's cross and celebrated in the Supper, is precisely that gift which can let the church be truthful. Best of all, the grace of Christ, offered in the Supper, is that which can forgive and heal those who have had abortions, or assisted or performed them, and who have then finally realized that they are guilty before the God who has created and owns all life.

## The Gifts of the Supper

When we consider the forgiveness and transformation of life that are offered through the means of this sacrament, it is no wonder that the Supper is often called a eucharist. That word comes from the Greek *euchoristo,* which means "thanksgiving," and certainly the church can only give thanks for what the grace of the Supper can mean in connection with abortion.

The gifts that are communicated to the church through this sacrament are given by the work of the Holy Spirit. Thus, every proper communion liturgy includes an *epiclesis,* a prayer for the Holy Spirit, which is often modeled on the words found in 1 Corinthians 10:16. For example:

> Gracious God, pour out your Holy Spirit upon us and upon these
> your gifts of bread and wine, that the bread we break and the cup

we bless may be the communion of the body and blood of Christ. By your Spirit make us one with Christ, that we may be one with all who share this feast, united in ministry in every place. As this bread is Christ's body for us, send us out to be the body of Christ in the world. (*The Book of Common Worship*, 1993)

It is by the work of the Holy Spirit that the real presence of Christ is communicated to the church in the Supper. He is the host at his table, and it is his life, his body, his blood, under the signs of bread and wine, that are given to the communicants, once again fulfilling his promise to be with his church through all time (Matt. 28:20). In the Supper, the church truly has communion with its Lord, and participates in his death and resurrection. Thus, the Lord's Supper reaffirms ever anew that victory over death that we discussed in connection with baptism.

The Supper is primarily the gift of life to us — of the new life of our Lord Jesus Christ. It is not just a mournful remembrance of his death, nor is it a reenactment of his sacrifice. Christ once and for all died on the cross and was raised from the grave and ascended in triumph, to rule at the right hand of his Father as the Lord of all (Phil. 2:9-11). And with that risen and ruling Lord we commune at the table, and in his new life we participate.

Can the church then in any way believe that it can acceptably approach the feast, bearing the dead bodies of aborted children? Not unless it wishes to eat and drink judgment upon itself (1 Cor. 11:27-29). Not unless it comes in deepest penitence, seeking transformation of its faithless life, and throws itself upon the mercy of the God in Christ who can make all things new (2 Cor. 5:17). There can be forgiveness at the Lord's table for the church's failure to take a stand against abortion, but only if the church is willing to surrender itself to its God in Christ, who wills life for us and not death. Indeed, the church's repentance and surrender will necessarily involve active commitment to those babies rescued from the certain death of abortion, through its own assurances that the community of believers will provide for those children, because it is so abundantly provided for by its Lord. In faith, the church will set about to "rescue the perishing."

## The Communion of the Saints

Because we participate in Christ through the means of the Lord's Supper and commune with him, we also commune with one another, and that too is of great significance in connection with the abortion issue.

The highest form of unity in the church is its common feast at the Lord's table, for we all partake of the one Loaf, which is the Body of Christ.

> Because there is one bread, we who are many are one body, for we all partake of the one bread. (1 Cor. 10:17)

We all eat the one Bread from heaven (cf. John 6:58), and we all drink the one cup of his blood. And in him, we are united together as one company of God's people, through the work of the Holy Spirit. As Helmut Thielicke once wrote, "The communion of saints does not consist in the fact that all of us say the same thing in the same words, but rather that we all drink from the same spring."[4]

There exists therefore within the communing body of the church a mutual forgiveness of one another, signified by the kiss of peace; a mutual concern for one another, signified by our service; a mutual responsibility to one another, signified by our ongoing concern for each others' lives. In the love of church members for one another, that love of God in Christ with which we are fed at the Supper, is visibly made manifest.

No other rite of the church therefore bears so much significance for our actions toward the pregnant woman in our midst. We are one with her in the Body of Christ, and we are one with the child whom she carries in her womb. We know that both she and her child belong to God in Christ, and that we have been joined together with her in the unity of the one Spirit, in which we feast together at the Lord's table (cf. Eph. 4:3). The church therefore protects and supports and prays for and helps child and mother and father, through the nine months of pregnancy. And when the child is born, the church rejoices at the safe passage of the child into the world, and takes him or her

---

4. Helmut Thielicke, *Encounter with Spurgeon*, trans. John W. Doberstein (Grand Rapids: Baker Book House, 1963), pp. 44-45.

into its loving care, nurturing, baptizing, teaching, guiding, assuming further responsibility for this new Christian in its midst.

After telling the parable of the Good Samaritan, Jesus asks, "Which of these . . . do you think proved neighbor to the man who fell among the robbers?" The answer was, "The one who showed mercy on him." And Jesus replied, "Go and do likewise" (Luke 10:29-37). The question posed by the communion of the Lord's table is: "What sort of neighbor will the church be to a mother and her baby?"

Sometimes, of course, it is not easy for the Body of Christ to assume such responsibilities, especially when there is a so-called "problem pregnancy" — involving an unwed mother, a deformed or mentally retarded child, a poverty-stricken couple, an ashamed teenager. But those of us who participate in Christ's body and blood at the Lord's Supper, participate not only in his death and resurrection, but also in his suffering; we indicate our willingness to suffer with Christ, if need be, for the sake of all those whom he has loved, even unto death on the cross.

We commune with one another at the Supper, but that communion is not only with those present. It is also communion with the whole company of the church in all times and places: "with all the company of heaven," reads the Great Thanksgiving. We eat and drink with all the faithful who have gone before us — with Peter and Paul, with Augustine and Luther, with Calvin and Bonhoeffer and King, and yes, with our departed loved ones who have died in the faith. We celebrate with all those still living, wherever they be in the world, who share the one bread and drink the one cup that are our Lord Jesus Christ — with all those contemporary saints in the church to whom we look for leadership and guidance, and with the most ordinary Christian in the tiniest hamlet in Christ's kingdom. All these are present at the Supper with us, because all participate in Christ as we do, and we are joined with a vast "cloud of witnesses" spanning the ages and the globe.

## The Witness of the Saints

The communion of saints raises the question, however, of how we stand in that sacred company with regard to abortion. As we pointed out in the Introduction, the church has sanctioned abortion in its official policies only in the last twenty or thirty years. And so the modern church, with the blood of one and one-half million aborted children on its hands every year, eats and drinks in the Supper with, for example, Luther and Calvin, who leveled the most scorching condemnation against the practice of abortion. Has the church's memory on this issue become so short that it can commune with its forebears in the faith in good conscience? And can it ignore the prophetic and saintly voices within its midst in the present time who condemn the killing? Said Mother Teresa in 1986, when speaking of unwanted children who might be aborted, "If you don't want the child, give him to me. I want him."[5]

We are surrounded by a "great cloud of witnesses" at the Lord's Supper, whose testimony to us about abortion accords with what the church has said on the subject for nearly two thousand years. Given the weight of that tradition, and its consonance with the Scriptures, we ignore it at the peril of our souls.

> Therefore, since we are surrounded by so great a cloud of witnesses, let us also lay aside every weight, and sin which clings so closely, and let us run with perseverance the race that is set before us, looking to Jesus the pioneer and perfecter of our faith, who for the joy that was set before him endured the cross, despising the shame, and is seated at the right hand of the throne of God. (Heb. 12:1-2)

## Anticipation of the Kingdom

The Lord's Supper also looks forward eagerly to the coming of the kingdom of God. It deals with what the church calls "eschatology," with "knowledge of the end." The Synoptic Gospels record that at the last supper with his disciples, Jesus said, "I shall not drink again of the fruit of the vine until that day when I drink it new in the kingdom of God" (Mark 14:25 and parallels). Thus, that last supper in the upper room was a foretaste for Jesus and his disciples of a coming banquet,

5. In an address at a Presbyterian Pro-Life meeting at the General Assembly of the PCUSA, June 8, 1988, in St. Louis, Missouri.

of a messianic banquet, in the kingdom of God. And so too is the Lord's Supper a foretaste for us of that future fulfillment. We commune with our Lord at the Supper, knowing that such communion is the foretaste of a final communion when we shall all be with the Lord (1 Thess. 4:17), who will be praised as Ruler over all (1 Cor. 15:28; Rev. 11:15-17).

In the tradition handed down in the church to Paul, he records the faith of the church that, "As often as you eat this bread and drink the cup, you proclaim the Lord's death until he comes" (1 Cor. 11:26). Christ comes again to set up his kingdom on earth, and in the Supper, the church eagerly awaits that good coming. Thus, the eucharistic cry preserved for us by Paul and John is *Marantha!* "Our Lord, come!" (1 Cor. 16:22; Rev. 22:20; cf. Phil. 4:5).

That coming can mean judgment upon the church for its failure to save innocent unborn children and to succor their mothers.

> For we must all appear before the judgment seat of Christ, so that each one may receive recompense for what has been done in the body, whether good or evil. (2 Cor. 5:10 RSV; Matt. 16:27; Acts 10:42; 17:32; Rom. 2:16, etc.)

Our Lord tells us that what we have done to "the least of these" who are members of his family, we have done to him (Matt. 25:40, 45 NRSV).

The coming of our Lord to bring in his kingdom can also mean great hope for the communing church, however, for the Scriptures teach that God's final work with this world will be its total transformation into "a new heaven and a new earth," when God himself — the Father, Son, and Holy Spirit — will be with us. And he will wipe away every tear from our eyes, and death shall be no more, neither shall there be mourning nor crying nor pain any more, for the former things will have passed away (Rev. 21:3-4). In other words, the sin that is abortion will be no more, and the trauma suffered by the women who have had abortions will never again be experienced. To add to the joy, stillborn children, spontaneous abortions, the birth of handicapped and deformed children — all those results of our common fallen condition — will be pains of the past. And our suffering world will know the goodness, the wholeness, the abundant life that God intended for us at the beginning, when first he created everything and pronounced it "very good" (Gen. 1:31).

## What Sorts of Persons?

As 2 Peter says, however, since all these things will come to pass, what sorts of persons ought we to be, waiting for the coming of the Lord (3:11-12)? The church is the communion of the "kingdom people," those who at the Supper participate in the risen body of their Lord, those who are given bread and drink for their pilgrimage toward the kingdom, those who taste with that bread and wine the first fruits of God's final reign. Should our lives, then, not reflect the character of that final destination? Should we in the church not be working *now* to end the sinful killing of the innocent that brings judgment on our society?

Certainly in the Great Prayer of Thanksgiving, the *epiclesis* or prayer for the Holy Spirit is followed by the *oblation*, in which we dedicate ourselves to the purposes of God's kingdom.

> Here we offer ourselves to be a living sacrifice, holy and acceptable to you. In your mercy, accept our sacrifice of praise and thanksgiving. In communion with all the faithful in heaven and on earth, we ask you to fulfill, in us and in all creation, the purpose of your redeeming love.[6]

So too the prayer of thanksgiving at the end of the communion service emphasizes our dedication to live in accord with God's coming kingdom. For example, this is the closing prayer from the Scots *Book of Common Order, 1979:*

> Almighty and ever-living God, we thank thee that in thy great love thou hast fed us at thy table with this spiritual food and brought us into fellowship with thy whole Church in heaven and on earth, making us heirs through hope of thine everlasting kingdom.
>
> Send us out into the world in the power of thy Spirit, to live and to work to thy praise and glory: through thy Son Jesus Christ our Lord who liveth and reigneth with thee in the unity of the Holy Spirit, one God, world without end. Amen.

The Supper looks forward to the time when there will be no more suffering and death associated with abortion, and it nourishes us to

---

6. "The Service for the Lord's Day," *Supplemental Liturgical Resource 1* (Philadelphia: The Westminster Press, 1984), p. 105.

work in our present time for the elimination of that evil. As Hughes Old has written, "One should not overlook . . . that for Christ to abide in our hearts implies that he rules in our hearts."[7] Thus the gift of Christ's life to his church at the Lord's Supper is a constant challenge for the church to work for life for all persons, born and unborn. Above all, the Supper is an ongoing challenge to the church to put its own house in order by rejecting the nihilism of abortion.

7. *Worship* (Atlanta: John Knox Press, 1984), p. 134.

# CHAPTER 5

# *The Supper and the Christian Life*

At the Lord's Supper, as at Israel's first covenant ceremony with its God, the church pledges itself to live as God's "peculiar treasure" (Exod. 19:5 KJV), as his "own possession among all peoples" (RSV). The church is the new Israel in Jesus Christ (Gal. 6:16), and so like the Israel of old, we promise to follow all the commandments that our Lord has given us. "All that the Lord has spoken, we will do, and we will be obedient" (Exod. 24:7; cf. 19:5).

The Bible expresses this uniquely Christian way of life by saying that we in the church are a "holy nation" (1 Pet. 2:9; Exod. 19:6); we are a people set apart for the purposes of God. That is the meaning of the word "holy" in the Scriptures, when applied to human beings. The root meaning of the verb *qadash*, "to be holy," in the Hebrew, or *hagiadzo* in the Greek, is "to cut," or "to separate." Thus, when the Scriptures tell us that the church is a "holy nation," they are not saying that we are morally pure; all of us daily have to confess our sins before Almighty God. Rather, the Scriptures are saying that the church is that people whom God has set apart for his purpose, and whose life is to be ordered and governed by the will of God and not by the will of human beings. And when we partake of the Lord's Supper, entering into covenant with him, as his "kingdom people," we pledge ourselves to that obedience.

> Not every one who says to me, "Lord, Lord," shall enter the kingdom of heaven, but he who does the will of my Father who is in heaven. (Matt. 7:21)

65

Indeed, the entire Sermon on the Mount in Matthew 5–7, is intended as Christ's instructions for the church, the new people of God who participate in the powers of the new age by their participation in the life of their Lord. And chapter after chapter of the New Testament marks out the path which Christians are to walk, by the power of the Spirit of Christ, in their new life of obedience (cf. e.g. Gal. 5:16–6:10).

## The Nature of the Christian Life

The Christian life has nothing to do with unbridled freedom in the use of our sexuality or, for that matter, in the use of any other gift God has given us. To be totally free, says Paul, is to live under God's wrath, to be loosed from his loving hand, and to be given over to sin's captivity, just to wallow in it (Rom. 1:18-32). And so Jesus bids us, "Take my yoke upon you, and learn from me . . . and you will find rest for your souls. For my yoke is easy, and my burden is light" (Matt. 11:29-30). The Christian life means wearing a yoke and being guided in "paths of righteousness" (Ps. 23:3) by the reins of a loving Master.

The prophet Jeremiah gives us a vivid picture of what the people of God become when they cast off that "easy" yoke:

> . . . long ago you broke your yoke,
>   and burst your bonds;
> and you said, "I will not serve." . . .
> Look at your way in the valley;
>   know what you have done —
> a restive young camel interlacing her tracks,
>   a wild ass used to the wilderness,
> in her heat sniffing the wind!
>   Who can restrain her lust?
>
> (Jer. 2:20, 23-24)

We become like beasts apart from the guiding commands of God, Jeremiah is saying, and the prophet uses shocking sexual figures to make the point. But are the figures not appropriate to a society like ours that is so obsessed with unbridled sex that it can idolize someone like Madonna or exhibit photos of sadistic sex in an art gallery?

We now live in a culture in the United States in which almost any sexual expression or action is deemed acceptable. Indeed, sexuality has become, in many peoples' minds, *the* defining characteristic of personhood, and many persons now believe that they cannot be whole persons unless they exercise their sexuality, whether they be single, married, or homosexual. They are thereby saying, of course, that Jesus of Nazareth was not a whole person, but such is the obstinate degradation of our society.

The results we have reaped are no less horrible than those pictured by Jeremiah: epidemics of AIDS and other venereal diseases; babies born to unwed teenagers; broken homes with their resulting poverty; child abuse; pornography; the collapse of all moral standards; and finally, the slaughter of thirty million unborn children by abortion since 1973. No, the Christian life has nothing to do with that so-called "sexual freedom."

Christians, who partake of the Lord's Supper, do not live by the standards of society around them. The people of the old covenant were never to live that way.

> And the Lord said to Moses, "Say to the people of Israel, I am the Lord your God. You shall not do as they do in the land of Egypt, where you dwelt, and you shall not do as they do in the land of Canaan, to which I am bringing you. You shall not walk in their statutes. You shall do my ordinances and keep my statutes and walk in them. I am the Lord your God. (Lev. 18:2-4)

Nor do the people of the new covenant that is celebrated in the Lord's Supper follow society's ways.

> Do not be conformed to this world but be transformed by the renewal of your mind, that you may prove what is the will of God, what is good and acceptable and perfect. (Rom. 12:2)

"This world" knows nothing about what it means to be redeemed, to be forgiven, to be granted a new life and given a mission and set on a pilgrimage toward "a city that has foundations, whose builder and maker is God" (Heb. 11:10). It is still lost in the darkness of sin and knows nothing of that gospel. But the people of God know, and so they walk by the light of a Word shining in the darkness, which the darkness cannot extinguish (John 1:5), and they are sustained by the "living bread which came down from heaven" (John 6:51) and on which they have feasted in the Supper.

In short, having been given the Spirit of Christ by whose power it is able to be obedient, the church dedicates itself at its eucharist, its covenant renewal ceremony, to walk by God's commandments alone. "Follow me," Jesus commands, and the feasting church replies, "We will."

## The Function of the Commandments

Obedience to God's commandments concerning sex, given us in the Scriptures, is not a form of legalism or works righteousness on the part of the church. We are not working our way into relationship with our God by obeying his commandments, any more than was Israel at Mt. Sinai. God had already redeemed her from slavery and adopted her as his child, long before he gave her the covenant Ten Commandments. God had already borne her on eagles' wings and brought her to himself (Exod. 19:4). And so too, God has already redeemed us by the cross of Christ and adopted us as his own in our baptism, long before we have responded in obedience. "While we were yet sinners Christ died for us" (Rom. 5:8), and the benefits of that death have then been conveyed to us through the Word and sacraments.

Our obedience to God's commandments about sex is therefore our grateful *response* to what God has done for us. This merciful God does not redeem us and then just let us stumble around in the dark, trying to decide how to live our new lives in Christ. No. God continues to love us by showing the way. He continues to go with us, to guide our paths, to prevent us from falling into temptation and error. "Lead us not into temptation," we pray in the Lord's prayer, "and deliver us from evil" (Matt. 6:13), and God answers that prayer by giving us guidance in his commandments.

In short, the commandments of God about our sexual lives are not legalistic requirements laid upon us in order that we can win God's favor. They are part of the merciful guidance granted to us by a God in whose favor we already live, because of the work of Jesus Christ. The law, writes John Calvin,

68

> is the best instrument for enabling [believers in whose hearts the Spirit of God already flourishes and reigns] to learn with greater truth and certainty what the will of the Lord is which they aspire to follow, and to confirm them in this knowledge. . . . By frequently meditating on the law [the servant of God] will be excited to obedience, and confirmed in it, and so drawn away from the slippery paths of sin.[1]

We obey those commandments out of gratitude for all God has already done for us, and because we know that he loves us and wants us to have abundant life, free of sin. "Oh that they had such a mind as this always," God yearns in Deuteronomy, "to fear me and to keep all my commandments, that it might go well with them and with their children for ever" (Deut. 5:29). God wants it to go well with us. God loves us and wants us and our children to live (cf. Ezek. 18:32). And so in his mercy he continues to guide us by means of his commandments.

God's commandments for our sexual life, given us in the Scriptures, are therefore his merciful directions for abundant life in our sexual relations with one another. For example, when God commands, "You shall not commit adultery," that is a merciful gift of God, given us out of his love, because God knows that no one can have a joyful and abundant life in a marriage where adultery is practiced. We repeat: God loves us and wants it to go well with us, and so he gives us commandments by which we may know how to walk. And were the church to follow those commandments, and to teach them to its children and to all in society, the incidence of abortion in the United States would be greatly reduced.

## The Biblical View of Sex and Marriage

It is quite clear throughout the Scriptures that sex is a good gift of a loving God, intended to join husband and wife in the joyful union of one flesh (Gen. 2:24-25). The Bible emphasizes the goodness of the body, of the desire of male and female for one another, and of the resulting family (Gen. 2:23; cf. Ps. 127:3-5; 128:3-4; Prov. 30:18-19; Eccles. 9:9).

1. *Institutes of the Christian Religion* (London: James Clarke and Co., Ltd., 1949), 1.309.

But it is also clear throughout the Scriptures that sex is given only for the marital union of male and female, and that it is to be exercised only within the context of that union. Fornication, premarital and extra-marital sexual relations are all condemned in the Scriptures (Matt. 15:19; Mark 7:21; Gal. 5:19; Eph. 5:3, 5), as are seduction, rape, sodomy, bestiality, incest, prostitution, and homosexuality (Lev. 18; 19:20-22, 29; 20:10-21; Rom. 1:26-27; 1 Cor. 6:9). Modern attempts to find some warrant in Scripture for any of these practices are simply sinful self-delusions and rationalizations for faithlessness.

Similarly, throughout the Bible, marriage is intended to be a life-long, faithful relation of love, mutual helpfulness, and self-sacrifice (Gen. 2:18; Eph. 5:21-33). Divorce, which leaves so many impoverished and broken-hearted and so many children without a parent, is not the intention of God (Mal. 2:16; Mark 10:1-12 and parallels; 1 Cor. 7:10-16).[2]

There can be no doubt that many abortions are attempts to solve the problems raised when these commandments of God with regard to our sexual lives are broken. According to numerous surveys, the majority of abortions in the United States are obtained by white women under the age of twenty-five who have never been married and who have never had a child. In short, the sexual revolution of the 1960s has led to widespread sexual promiscuity within our society.

In December 1992, the president-elect of the Planned Parenthood Federation of America, Pamela Maraldo, was quoted in the news as saying, "Abortion is where the rubber hits the road, the line in the sand for women to become fully equal citizens."[3] What she implied was that "emancipated" women now have the same freedom as men to engage in unbridled sexual activity, because if they become pregnant, they can then dispose of the child by having an abortion: so-called "free" women can relieve themselves of all moral responsibility by killing their unborn children! It is no wonder that PPFA was described in the December 11, 1989, issue of *Time* magazine as "the premiere institution performing abortions in the country." Its fifty-

2. See Elizabeth Achtemeier, *The Committed Marriage* (Philadelphia: The Westminster Press, 1976). Also *Preaching About Family Relationships* (Philadelphia: The Westminster Press, 1987).
3. *Richmond Times-Dispatch*, Dec. 13, 1992.

seven affiliates performed 129,155 abortions in 1990 and over a million abortions between 1980 and 1990.[4]

Christians, by way of contrast, pledge themselves at the Lord's Supper to lead lives different from those of the sexually promiscuous, different from those who are willing to kill unborn children in order to be "free" to do what they want. Christians at the eucharist renew their covenant with their Lord and promise to walk in his ways and to obey his commands, by the power of the Holy Spirit, in the redeemed, new life that their God has granted them.

George Will once wrote a column in *Newsweek* magazine in which he recalled a statement of Charles Peguy's that "the true revolutionaries in our society are the parents of Christian families."[5] That is absolutely true! Christian family life is so different from the so-called family life practiced in the society around us that it is indeed revolutionary. And that has always been true of Christians. Thus the first century letter of 1 Peter remarks on the Christians' new lifestyle:

> Let the time that is past suffice for doing what the Gentiles like to do, living in licentiousness, passions, drunkenness, revels, carousing, and lawless idolatry. They are surprised that you do not now join them in the same wild profligacy, and they abuse you; but they will give account to him who is ready to judge the living and the dead. (1 Pet. 4:3-5)

As George Will further wrote, "Christianity is a religion of unadjusted people whose obligation is to adjust to something that transcends the culture of the day, any day."[6] Christians are persons who are called to adjust their lives to the lordship of God in Jesus Christ, and we can only confess that Christ is our Lord if we are willing to obey his commandments, including his commandments about our sexual practice. Jesus affirmed, as do all the Scriptures, that God's intention for our sexual practice is that it be limited to a lifelong, faithful, monogamous relationship between wife and husband (Mark 10:6-9; cf. Eph. 5:31). And no matter what others say, if the Christian Church emphasized

---

4. From a Service Report of the Planned Parenthood Foundation of America (1991), p. 10.

5. October 15, 1979, p. 140.

6. Ibid.

that in our society, and taught it and preached it and practiced it, there would be created within our country a moral climate that would reduce the number of abortions.

## The Church's Crisis of Faith

The difficulty is that many churches in our time have lost faith in the power of their own message. They no longer believe that the Christian gospel can influence or transform society in any way. They no longer believe that God's Word will not return to him void, but will accomplish that which God purposes, and prosper in the thing for which he sent it (Isa. 55:11). Much of the sexual and abortion crisis in the United States is due to a crisis of faith in the church.

The result is that many in the church now take it for granted that most young people will indulge in pre-marital sex. And the church therefore designs its educational materials accordingly, sometimes even counseling young people to practice "safe sex" and handing out condoms. This is an excerpt from the Majority Report on Abortion, adopted by the 204th General Assembly of the Presbyterian Church (USA) in 1992:

> Much as we might wish it otherwise, the church recognizes that sexual activity happens outside the marriage relationship. Thus the church continues to proclaim to the world the importance of love, respect for our partner, self-respect and equality, mutual support, fidelity, and the use of contraceptives.[7]

There is not a word in there to the effect that sexual activity "outside the marriage relationship" is a violation of God's commandments and a sin against him. But by such omissions, the church has forfeited its role as a moral guide and acquiesced to the social climate around it, in the belief that it is being "realistic." That it is also being unfaithful seems never to be an issue.

Similarly, many pastors now sanction homosexuality as a lifestyle acceptable to God, despite Old and New Testament admonitions

---

7. *Reports to the 204th General Assembly 1992*, 27.110.

against it. Or in counseling sessions dealing with marital problems, many pastors do not try to heal a troubled marriage or point out the teaching of Scripture. Rather, they assure the divorcing couple that no sin is involved; some denominations even have "worship services" that liturgically confirm divorce. It is no wonder, then, that some churches also sanction abortion, for such sanction is at one with the church's general abandonment of the merciful moral guides of the Scriptures.

Rather than converting the world, the church has succumbed to the world's ways. And so the Word is not rightly preached, and the Supper is not received in faith, and the church has lost its characteristic marks as the church of Jesus Christ because, as the Scriptures make quite clear, moral practice is part and parcel of worship, always affecting one's relationship with God.

No one makes this case better than the prophets of the Old Testament. For example, Isaiah 1:10-17 tells us that the people of his day in the eighth century B.C. loved to worship. They literally trampled the courts of the temple (v. 12), as crowds might in our churches on Christmas and Easter Sundays. But God declared that he hated it all:

> Your new moons and your appointed feasts
>     my soul hates;
> they have become a burden to me,
>     I am weary of bearing them.
> When you spread forth your hands [i.e. in prayer],
>     I will hide my eyes from you;
> even though you make many prayers,
>     I will not listen;
>     your hands are full of blood.

(vv. 14-15)

We have the naive belief that God hears every prayer, but not according to this passage from Isaiah. Why not? Because Judah's hands, lifted up in prayer to the Lord, are covered with the blood of the innocent poor (cf. v. 17). And our hands are equally smeared with the blood of millions of aborted children.

Jeremiah 7:1-15, probably dating to 609 B.C., tells us that the people thought of their place of worship as a "den of robbers," that is, as a place where they could *hide* from the consequences of their wrong-doing, and our Lord Jesus made the same accusation, according to the gospel writers (Mark 11:17 and parallels), when he cleansed the Jerusalem temple. But the prophet leveled God's judgment upon the nation of Judah for its duplicitous worship:

> Will you steal, murder, commit adultery, swear falsely, burn incense to Baal, and go after other gods that you have not known, and then come and stand before me in this house, which is called by my name, and say, "We are delivered!" — only to go on doing all these abominations? . . . I will cast you out of my sight. (vv. 9-10, 15)

God is of purer eyes than to behold evil and cannot look on wrong, says Habakkuk the prophet (1:13). He will not accept the worship of a people who deliberately defy his holy will.

Thus, the fifth-century B.C. prophet Malachi records that his people were covering the Lord's altar with tears, weeping, and groaning because God no longer accepted their offerings or looked on them with favor, and because they were suffering. But Malachi attributes God's disfavor to the Judeans' faithlessness in their marriage covenants (Mal. 2:13-16).

What we do in our ethics affects our worship of God. As Paul Hoon has written, "Liturgical action can be authentic only as the Christian man (or woman) is claimed to live out the commitments that illumine its meaning."[8] The church cannot sanction non-scriptural sexual relationships, and it cannot sanction abortion, while at the same time believing that it can practice baptism and commune at the Lord's Supper in integrity. Liturgy and life are connected, and they cannot be separated.

The church is therefore called in our day to preach the Word and to celebrate its sacraments rightly, and then it is sent by its Lord into the world to live a life commensurate with those marks of its life. If the Christian Church will do that, in the power of the Holy Spirit given to it, God's gospel will not return to him void, but it will accomplish that which he purposes and prosper in the thing for which he sent it (Isa. 55:11).

8. *The Integrity of Worship* (Nashville and New York: Abingdon Press, 1971), p. 327.

# CHAPTER 6

# *The Church and the Hard Cases*

The U.S. Centers for Disease Control and Prevention report roughly 1.3 million abortions yearly, and Planned Parenthood, the world's largest abortion provider, reports a higher figure that has varied between 1.5 and 1.6 million in recent years.

Only a tiny number of abortions occur in cases of rape, incest, fetal deformity, and threat to the life of the mother. In our day, conditions of pregnancy that threaten a woman's life are exceedingly rare. The incidence of pregnancies resulting from the other three conditions ranges from one to fifteen percent.[1] Accurate figures are difficult to obtain, at least partly because they depend on the willingness of women to report the reasons for their abortions. By any measure, the numbers constitute only a small percentage of the total number of abortions.

Nevertheless, all these situations exist, and it is especially important that the church be able to speak and minister to each of them. While it has become almost a reflex action to think of abortion as a

---

1. One estimate comes from a *Family Planning Perspectives* 1987 survey of 1900 women who had obtained abortions. One percent reported that they sought the abortion as the "victim of rape or incest"; thirteen percent responded that the "fetus had a possible health problem." The women surveyed could give more than one reason for their abortions, and the mean number of reasons given was nearly four. The most common response (seventy-six percent) was "Woman is concerned about how having a baby could change her life." Published in New York by the Alan Guttmacher Institute, Vol. 20, No. 4 (July/August 1988), pp. 169-170.

solution in these "hard" cases, we hope to show that there are more important considerations that apply. It is important for the church to explore exactly what creates the crisis in these pregnancies and then consider how it can minister effectively as Christ's body to those involved.


# Rape

Conception as a result of rape is a rare occurrence. But rape itself is not rare. In 1982, the FBI Uniform Crime Reports stated that there were 78,770 forcible rapes committed. By 1991 that number had swelled to 106,593. Furthermore, estimates of unreported rapes increase the incidence to between 40 and 80 percent more than the reported numbers.

In their 1979 study, entitled *Rape: Crisis and Recovery,*[2] Drs. Ann Wolbert Burgess and Lynda Lytle Holmstrom differentiate between "blitz rape," in which the victim is violently and suddenly attacked unawares, often by a complete stranger, and "confidence rape," in which the victim is lured into the situation by an assailant known to her, or by her initial trust in the assailant or assailants. Women have been brutally beaten, and even killed, in these assaults.

Rape produces trauma completely independent of pregnancy, and the church that wants to help must become educated about the effects on women who have been subjected to such violence. That is part of the process of learning how to "bear one another's burdens . . ." (Gal. 6:2).

Victims of such assaults often tell horror stories of the callousness, indifference, or accusatory attitudes with which they are treated by the police, hospitals, family members, friends, clergy and fellow Christians. The church must learn how to minister to and not add to that horror.


# The Trauma of Rape

The destructive effect of rape on a woman can scarcely be overstated. Burgess and Holmstrom asked victims to rate the effect of

2. (Bowie, Md: Robert J. Brady Co., 1979).

rape on a scale of 1 to 10, and these were some of the responses they received:

> You're never the same after it. You never return to that peace of mind of being safe. . . . I'd rank it 8 or 9 . . . certain parts never go away . . . it's very hard to deal with. (Rape victim, age 22)

> I'd rank it a 10 . . . it was the most scary, shocking thing that ever happened to me. (Rape victim, age 24)

> I'd rank it a 10 . . . or even higher than your top number, a 12 or 15. Worst thing that ever happened. Equal to the death of a spouse . . . takes away all security. (Rape victim, age 25)

The primary reaction of the victim at the time of the attack is fear of death or of bodily mutilation, and the trauma experienced is long-lasting and totally disrupting. Those who survive physically intact often carry a sense of death with them. One woman remarked that rape is never a one time trauma. It is repeated again and again when the memory is stimulated, involuntarily, by a particular odor, or color, or object. Studies show that nearly eighty percent of rape victims need four to six years to recover their former, normal way of life.[3]

Considering the nature of some attacks, the length of time required for recovery is not surprising. By threatening the victim with a weapon capable of causing death or mutilation, the rapist puts the woman completely at his mercy, and subjects her to horrifying abuse. One-fourth of all rapists force their victims to engage in oral (fellatio) or anal sex. Some women are subjected to cunnilingus. Victims report that the rapists urinated or masturbated on them, inserted objects into their vaginas, or forced them to dance, accompanying the acts with the most degrading language in order to humiliate them.

Immediate reactions after the rape may range from traumatic silence to hysterical crying, but all victims report a loss of all sense of self-control and self-confidence. They lose their basic trust in themselves and in others. Nausea and localized pain are common experi-

3. Helen Benedict, *Recovery: How to Survive Sexual Assault for Women, Men, Teenagers, Their Friends and Families* (Garden City, New York: Doubleday and Company, 1985), p. 35.

ences. The fear of being alone sets in, often accompanied by flash-backs of the attack, by depression, loss of sleep and appetite, night-mares, phobias, physical ills, and irrational self-blame.

Relationships of friendship, intimacy and trust are severely af-fected, as are ordinary social and working relationships. Over months and even years, victims may find that they can no longer handle their jobs or carry on their accustomed normal relationships, or return to normal sexual practices. Dr. Deborah Rose, a clinical professor in the Department of Psychiatry at Stanford University, described victims' reactions this way:

> Victims are profoundly mistrustful of all other people, even though the victim can recognize that others are trying to be suppor-tive and do care. . . . The old intrapsychic world is gone. . . . States of intrusive thoughts, feelings, and actions alternate with psychic numbing and a feeling of deadness. Intense fear of going crazy is present.
>
> [A competent woman in a responsible job can become] a cower-ing person on disability who is awake every night on the living room sofa, a can of Mace in her hand, waiting for the rapist to reappear, although he is in county jail awaiting trial, having been apprehended less than 12 hours after the assault. Only thoughts related to the rape now go through her mind and it's more than a year since the rape.
>
> Victims may experience a loss of sexual identity and sexuality and feel dirty, sullied, ruined, spoiled.[4]

Although medical action to end a possible pregnancy resulting from a rape is frequently automatic, Mahkorn's study of women who became pregnant as a result of sexual assault found that 27 of 38 who were seen by pregnancy-support counselors chose to continue their pregnancies. Some of the women cited beliefs that abortion involved violence, killing, or was immoral. Others expressed a belief in an intrin-sic meaning to human life. "One pregnant victim related that she felt she would suffer more mental anguish by taking the life of the child."[5]

4. *The Stanford Observer,* Nov. 1986, p. 11.
5. Sandra Kathleen Mahkorn, M.D. and William V. Dolan, M.D., "Sexual As-sault and Pregnancy," *New Perspectives on Human Abortion,* ed. Horan Hilgers and Frederick Mall, M.D. (University Publications of America, 1981), p. 189.

Those who study the effects of rape point out that the attention a woman receives following the attack can intensify her feeling of being victimized or can help her begin to regain her confidence in people. Medical personnel who disregard her feelings and decisions as irrational, and act instead entirely on their own judgment, tend to confirm the loss of control she just experienced in the rape.

Researchers and counselors have found that in order to recover from the trauma of rape, a woman must be able to face and talk about the attack, regain some sense of confidence and well-being, and feel that she is once again safe and able to meet the ordinary demands of her life. Many women find release only by moving to another city or residence.

## The Church's Role

The sacramental community of the church can have a significant role in assisting the recovery of a woman who has suffered the trauma of rape. The psychological and physical injury has also a spiritual component that professionals often overlook and are often ill equipped to minister to. The Body of Christ is equipped by its Lord to provide a restorative ministry in the lives of such women. There are things that the church should and should *not* do.

Pastors and church members should neither harbor nor express suspicions that the woman "asked for it," that she must have dressed or acted in a manner that awakened the sexual lust of the attacker, or that she is the type of woman who invites attack. A rape victim may already blame herself irrationally for the attack. She needs assurance that she is among people who trust her.

The church should become for her a welcoming community that receives her warmly into its midst as one of its own. If she is alone, church members can help restore her ability to trust other human beings by the warmth of their own presence in her life. They can offer her companionship, so that she does not have to be alone again until she is ready.

Friends, pastors, and adult family members should be willing to listen to details of the attack, no matter how shocking to their moral sensibilities. The victim needs to verbalize the experience, face it —

79

*when she is ready* — and come to terms with it, so she can triumph over it.

Those who listen should never suggest "what you should have done." Nor should listeners try to direct the victim's recovery. A woman who has been raped has lost her sense of self-control, and to tell her what to do is to deepen that loss. Friends can suggest alternatives for action, but the decisions must be made by the one hurt, not by someone else.

The church should not offer false assurances: that everything will be all right, that the victim's fears are groundless, that no harm has been done because the victim shows no sign of the attack and has survived. In fact, great harm has been done. The woman has been seriously threatened with death. Her fears are very real; they need to be heard and taken seriously.

And the church should not assume that medical and psychological treatment will meet all the needs of the rape victim. While the rape victim needs the same professional help as is proper for any other case of assault, the ministry of the Holy Spirit has the power to bind up her wounds and transform her life. Our Lord can minister with his own suffering to her overwhelming sense of injustice. God's word can teach her that there is no power in heaven or on earth that can bring down the one who is in Christ, for we are more than conquerors through him who loved us (Rom. 8:37).

The church can help the woman to do much better than cope with the tragedy that has befallen her. It can help her overcome it through a knowledge and experience of the sovereignty and merciful grace of God.

Jesus' parable of the Good Samaritan (Luke 10) teaches us that servants of God do not "pass by on the other side." They are the neighbors who lift the broken and the "half-dead" and see to it that they get the help they need for their healing. The community of baptized believers who find their own nourishment at the Lord's table, are called to be the tangible expression of God's succor, love and comfort, by drawing the one who has been harmed into the midst of their community.

The church also must live out its confidence in the transforming power of the gospel by being willing to administer God's mercy and grace to the rapist whenever it has opportunity, by calling him to confession and repentance and by believing that his life, too, can be redeemed.

## When a Pregnancy Results From Rape

Burgess and Holmstrom report that only three to five percent of forcible rapes result in pregnancy.[6] Some seventy-five percent of rapists have been shown to have some sexual dysfunction which prevents erection, penetration, or ejaculation.[7] Factors related to the victim also minimize the possibility of pregnancy: sterility, a previous hysterectomy, the use of contraceptives, an already existing pregnancy (in one study of 117 victims, 49 were already pregnant at the time of the assault); victims may be postmenopausal or may not yet have reached menarche, or may not have ovulated.[8]

The almost automatic assumption of our society is that every child conceived by rape should be aborted, and often the church has acquiesced in that assumption. But if abortion were the rule in rape, we would have lost beloved members of our communities.

To cite one example,[9] wife and mother Angie Bloedorn tells her story of being raped violently on a wintry night in a parking lot and of deciding to carry her baby to term and to raise the child as a beloved member of her family. Everyone closest to her counseled against the decision, including her doctor, her co-workers, and family members.

> . . . My sister chided me for "not getting rid of the problem"; my own mother actually told me I was out of my mind to have this baby. "If you *really* were raped, why don't you just have an abortion?" she asked. Her insinuation wounded me deeply.[10]

But Angie had experienced the trauma of an earlier abortion. More important, her husband Wally supported her decision to accept the baby as a member of their family

6. Burgess and Holmstrom, *Rape: Crisis and Recovery*, p. 114.
7. Ibid., p. 444.
8. Mahkorn and Dolan, *Sexual Assault and Pregnancy*, p. 189.
9. *ALL About Issues*, published by the American Life League (July-August, 1993).
10. Ibid., p. 25.

... My worst fear during the whole ordeal was that Wally would not be able to accept and love her. Nothing could be further from the truth. He's crazy about her! As soon as he gets home from work, he scoops up Hannah in his arms. . . . I'm not glad I was raped — not for a minute, but I am glad that we have this precious new life in our family. People ask me how I could bear to keep my rapist's baby. I tell them that I don't see her as *his* baby. She's *my* baby.[11]

Most important of all, however, Angie sees her baby, not from her own perspective, but from God's, and she accepts her baby as God's gift.

God has a plan for her, in spite of how her life began. He has a special reason for this child. . . . Through this whole experience, I've learned that God can bring good out of the most terrible situations — even something as terrible as rape.[12]

A message of the Christian Church is embodied in that simple statement. God is able to bring good out of the most horrible evil; the prime example of that is the cross of Christ. When everything looks hopeless to us, when nothing lies ahead but a crucifixion, when we would do almost anything to avoid its torture, and we cry out, "Remove this cup from me!" God yet has a resurrection planned in the future.

God does not will the evil of rape. That violence is solely the result of human sin. But God can take a child of rape and give him or her a future. For two thousand years our most dreadful and sinful deeds have not thwarted God from working out his plan to bring in his kingdom. And the children conceived in rape are not outside his plan. God promises that if we will trust his working, he will support and guide us all along the way — giving us strength when we have none; stilling our fears when we are overcome with terror; lending hope when all hope seems lost.

A pregnancy resulting from rape may be a terrible shock; but it is also an opportunity to restore life in the midst of a situation that carries with it the stench of death. A woman's decision to bear the child of rape is a decision of enormous faith and courage. The body of Christ has no reason to hope for the preservation of a life begun by a rape

11. Ibid.
12. Ibid.

unless it is willing to bring hope into the life of the woman who has none. Those of us who have truly received nourishment from the Lord's table have ourselves experienced the victory of life over death. We are those able to minister life and hope to others.

> Blessed be the God and Father of our Lord Jesus Christ, the Father of mercies and the God of all consolation, who consoles us in all our affliction, so that we may be able to console those who are in any affliction with the consolation with which we ourselves are consoled by God. (2 Cor. 1:3, 4 NRSV)

## The Church and Incest

Reliable statistics on the incidence of incest are not available. But it is important to keep the problem of incest in perspective. One survey of adolescents, aged 18-22, found that seven percent reported having been "forced to have sex against your will, or being raped."[13] It goes without saying that most children are not growing up in sexually abusive families; nevertheless, when incest occurs, it is a profoundly serious sin of one family member against another.

Incest rarely involves the physical violence and threat of death associated with rape. Instead, the victim is usually coerced verbally by some relative whom he or she has loved or respected or regarded as an authority figure. Incest is a terrible violation of trust within a family circle.

The incestuous relative already has a position of power over the victim, and the aim is usually to gain sexual arousal or satisfaction. However, there can be multiple reasons for an incestuous attack. In February of 1993, USA TODAY published this brief news story:

> The mother and father of a 15-year old girl in Fort Pierce, Fla., were accused of coercing her to have sex with [her father] in hopes she

---

13. From the National Survey of Children (NSC), Cycle III of the National Survey of Family Growth (NFG) and the National Longitudinal Surveys of Labor Force Behavior of Youth (NLSY), reported in an article entitled "Nonvoluntary Sexual Activity Among Adolescents," *Family Planning Perspectives*, Vol. 21, No. 3 (May/June 1989), pp. 110-111.

would conceive a child the parents are unable to bear. The parents
. . . are charged with sexual battery, which in Florida is the same as
rape. The girl said she agreed to have the baby in exchange for her
parents' permission to marry. She did not get pregnant.

Experts tell us that ninety percent of incest cases involve fathers
and their daughters, and one-third of the approximately one million
cases every year involve members of the child's immediate family.[14]
Incestuous relationships that start when the child is very small and
end with puberty only rarely involve penetration. However, incestuous
relationships may begin at puberty and continue until the young victim leaves home. Case workers report that incest is one of the three
primary reasons that children of both sexes run away from their
homes.[15]

Incestuous relatives often try to convince the young victims that
they will "like" the fondling and sex involved. Some incestuous fathers
regard their daughters as substitute wives or lovers, and lay the blame
for the relationship on an "inadequate" or "bad" wife.

Incest victims almost unanimously report feelings of terror, dis-
gust, and pain accompanying the abuse. They are trapped in the situation, however, until they become old enough to resist successfully,
to seek help, or to run away. Often other family members will not
believe their reports of what is happening, and running away or turning to a rape crisis center or trusted friend becomes their only avenue
of escape.

When the incestuous relationship results in pregnancy, the attacker often will deny the relationship, subjecting his young victim to
the charge of promiscuity, or will arrange for a secret abortion, adding
further to her distress and trauma.

As with rape, the church needs to learn all it can about incest in
order to minister effectively. Therefore, a relationship with a good rape
or family crisis center, which has a Christian world view, may be important in the church's development of understanding of and ministry
to the problem.

A principal distinction between rape and incest is the devastating

14. Benedict, *Recovery*, pp. 203-204.
15. Ibid., p. 202.

effect of incest on the whole family, and the whole family will need the church's ministry. The church's primary role is, through its Word and sacraments, to bring forth new creations, new persons, in Jesus Christ, who covenant to live no longer according to the world's ways but henceforth to live lives obedient to their Lord.

The church has an important role in the preventive help it can offer with its preaching and teaching ministry, and in the encouragement that comes from its own sacramental life to develop strong Christian families. In our sex-saturated culture where families form, break up, and reform, and where biblical standards of sexual practice are repudiated, incestuous relationships are an increasing temptation.

The preaching and teaching ministry of the church ought to establish sexual moorings for both parents and children. The sacramental life of the church ought to be a safe haven of help for those fleeing incest. The church ought to be a community of healing for those affected by the sin, and to offer a ministry of redemption and restoration for the sinner.

The principal need in cases of incest involving mature teenagers and their fathers is a ministry aimed toward healing of the one sinned against and redemption for the perpetrator of the sin. Many pastors and church members are not trained to meet all the needs involved in this sort of family crisis, and they should not hesitate to seek out and refer the family to competent Christian counseling services. But always the church can be a community ministering spiritually to family members.

When pregnancy occurs from an incestuous relation, abortion is not the solution that it might seem. Abortion brings its own trauma and distressing after-effects to an incestuous relationship that results in pregnancy, and may only aggravate the situation by helping conceal the sinful family relationship.

A young woman, pregnant as the result of incest, surrounded by the loving, accepting body of the church, will have enormous obstacles to overcome, to be sure. It is another situation where the woman's decision may be affected by a demonstration by the people of God of their faith that God has a purpose and plan for each child he gives, and that God's plan includes bringing good out of the darkest experiences of our lives. The willingness of the sacramental community to welcome the family members into their fellowship, and to bear their burdens, may be the source of courage and strength the family needs to welcome the innocent new life into a situation overwhelmed by guilt. "With God, all things are possible." God-given wisdom and an unswerving faith in God's ability to bring good out of evil may bring a happy result out of the tragedy of incest.

Incest can produce deep damage in the lives of those it touches. The church cannot hope to overcome its effects without relying on God's help, and without rolling up its sleeves in long-term commitment to a ministry of healing and discipline in the lives of those affected.

## Dealing with Fetal Deformity

> As he walked along, he saw a man blind from birth. His disciples asked him, "Rabbi, who sinned, this man or his parents, that he was born blind?" Jesus answered, "Neither this man nor his parents sinned; he was born blind so that God's works might be revealed in him. . . ." When he had said this, he spat on the ground and made mud with the saliva and spread the mud on the man's eyes, saying to him, "Go, wash in the pool of Siloam." Then he went and washed and came back able to see. (John 9:1-7 NRSV)

For centuries the unborn child remained "a medical recluse in an opaque womb."[16] Fetal development now can be observed by means of ultrasound pictures (sonography), which furnish a noninvasive technique that appears to be safe for both the unborn child and the mother.

Also until recently, when a malformation was discovered in the unborn child, the only options were either to abort the child or to await his or her delivery. Now many conditions can be corrected before birth. Most malformations that can be corrected by surgery, such as craniofacial, extremity, and chest wall deformities are best treated after birth, but there are some, such as urinary tract obstructions, that may interfere with the child's development and require surgical relief before birth. Other conditions, such as intrauterine growth retarda-

16. Michael R. Harrison, "Selection for Treatment: Which Defects are Correctable?" *The Unborn Patient*, ed. Michael R. Harrison, Mitchell S. Golbus, and Roy A. Filly (Philadelphia, W. B. Saunders, Co., 1991), pp. 159-165.

tion, cause progressive harm within the uterus and may require early delivery for repair, while others, such as hydrocephalus, may benefit from cesarean delivery. Some, such as anemia, can be treated in the uterus. Thus, modern medicine has greatly reduced the incidence of children born deformed or dead. There were 4,111,000 live births in this country in 1991; by contrast, only 8,670 infants died from conditions suffered in the prenatal period.[17] God has given us wonderful gifts in the advance of fetal treatment. And as long as the objective of medicine is to provide care and to restore, we can hope for continued advances in prenatal treatment.

Prenatal diagnosis is far from a perfect science, however. Many families that choose to continue their "high risk" pregnancies, some with the prayerful support of their churches, deliver babies with no perceptible problems, or problems of a minor, correctable nature. But diagnoses do not always miss the mark: families, trusting God within praying church communities, may deliver severely deformed or mentally retarded children. But the church ought not to regard that as an overwhelming tragedy. Dr. C. Everett Koop, the world famous pediatric surgeon and former Surgeon General of the United States, noted that in the more than thirty years that he practiced pediatric surgery, he never met a child with a birth defect who would have preferred to have his or her life terminated in utero rather than live with a handicap that might require multiple surgical procedures.[18] Further,

> more than one couple who were told that their baby would be born with a deformity or handicap and who have allowed the child to be born have stressed the positive impact that such a birth has had in drawing their family closer together and enabling them to experience a dimension of . . . love and compassion . . . that might not have occurred otherwise.[19]

Children do not have to be perfectly normal to bring blessing to

---

17. National Center for Health Statistics, U.S. Department of Health and Human Services.

18. C. E. Koop, *The Right to Live: The Right to Die* (Wheaton: Tyndale House Publishing, 1976).

19. Thomas A. Miller, *The Minority Report of the Special Committee on Problem Pregnancies and Abortion* (Presbyterian Church in the USA, 1992).

a family. The Fall is manifested in all of us. Those with eyes to see can acknowledge deficiencies in their own "normalcy" as they share the mercy and grace of God in the life of an especially needy baby.

Abortion as the sole solution for handicap raises the specter of eugenics. Rather than eliciting from us a tireless effort to find a means of healing for those we love and have welcomed into our community as heirs with us of God's promises, the abortion option tempts us to believe we can produce a world of perfect people, free of the effects of the Fall, by weeding out the imperfect. It deceives us into believing we have no responsibility to love and care for those who do not meet a standard of humanness of our own devising. It persuades us that we do not have the time, or resources, or strength to care for a human being whose contribution to the common good is so much less than our own. Abortion is a way of disowning the imperfect; it allows us to deny that the imperfect belong to us.

Jesus' own healing ministry teaches us to fight the effects of the Fall with determination to overcome handicaps and find their cures. That is the true legacy of the practice of medicine: never to harm, always to heal.

Who can see what blessing lies in store for the family who accepts the child God gives them? And who can see what blessing lies in store for the church that welcomes the weak and vulnerable into its fellowship through baptism and the Lord's Supper, surrounds them with the warmth of human contact and care? It is natural to life within Christ's body not only to accept each member as a gift from God, but also to pray and work for healing where there is illness, for wholeness where there is deformity, and for opportunities for those who remain weak and vulnerable to live lives as productively as possible and in all things to give praise and thanks to the God in whose image they are made and from whom their lives derive meaning and purpose.

The church is the fellowship that values all persons, no matter how deformed or repulsive they may appear to a society whose values are shaped by "beauty" and "usefulness." The church knows that handicapped persons are beloved in the sight of him who "had no form or comeliness that we should look at him, and no beauty that we should desire him." The Head of the church is the One who "was despised and rejected by men; a man of sorrows and acquainted with grief" (Isa. 53:2-3), and so those who know that Head know that he welcomes all children to himself.

Discipleship in this area of the church's life is not an easy solution to a problem pregnancy. It may involve both emotional and physical sweat and tears. But it is never marked by the despair that characterizes an abortion decision.

The church can give assistance to parents in the care of their disabled children, providing them with relief and substitutes, so the parents can take a break. The church can help identify the special needs of the handicapped and help search out how those needs may be met both within the church and in the community at large, whether the needs be medical, educational, vocational, emotional, spiritual or financial. But above all, the church can mediate the supporting love and succor and strength of its God through its human contact with the handicapped child, the parents and the family. The Lord of the church has proclaimed, "Fear not, for I am with you. . . . I will strengthen you, I will help you" (Isa. 41:10).

> When you pass through the waters I will be with you;
> and through the rivers, they shall not overwhelm you;
> when you walk through fire you shall not be burned,
> and the flame shall not consume you.
>
> (Isa. 43:2)

## Threat to the Life of the Mother

Some pregnancies may threaten the life of the mother, although modern medicine mercifully has made these instances rare when the woman has access to competent medical care. Thus, the church needs to be concerned for the prenatal care of every pregnant woman in its company. Some women may need transportation to a medical facility. Some may need financial assistance. Some may even need to be aided in ending unhealthy practices, such as the use of drugs and alcohol, that threaten both themselves and their unborn children. If a church is truly a communion of its Lord, it will be accountable for the physical as well as the spiritual needs of its members.

In many cases, women with life-threatening conditions may be able to continue a pregnancy with careful medical attention. There are rare occasions, however, when the doctors' objective to preserve both lives cannot be achieved. In some cases the mother's life is preserved at the cost of the baby's. There have been cases when the mother has relinquished her own life in order to preserve the life of her child. Abortion is never the objective in these cases; the objective is to preserve both lives and the sacrifice of one of the lives is a tragedy that the whole community mourns. In these cases the church is called to affirm the value of each life, to surround the family with its love and tangible support, and to pray for comfort from their merciful God in the lives of the bereaved.[20]

Though the "hard cases" actually account for very few abortions, they are indeed hard cases. Any family or individual who faces a pregnancy involving the situations discussed in this chapter has the opportunity to experience the faith expressed in the ministry of the church of Jesus Christ and to taste and see that the Lord is good, even — and especially — in the dark hours of life.

20. Chapter 3 mentions the "Service of Hope After Loss of Pregnancy" contained in the 1989 book of worship of the United Methodist Church.

# CHAPTER 7

# *Abortion and Church Discipline*[1]

The notes of the true kirk, therefore, we believe, confess and avow to be: first, the true preaching of the Word of God, in which he revealed himself to us, as the writings of the prophets and apostles declare; secondly, the right administration of the sacraments of Christ Jesus, with which must be associated the Word and promise of God to seal and confirm them in our hearts; and lastly, ecclesiastical discipline uprightly ministered, as God's Word prescribes, whereby vice is repressed and virtue nourished. (*The Scots Confession*, 18.3.18)

. . . since discipline is an absolute necessity in the Church, it also falls to ministers to regulate this discipline for edification. . . . At all times and in all places the rule is to be observed that everything is to be done for edification, decently and honorably, without oppression and strife. For the apostle testifies that authority in the Church was given to him by the Lord for building up and not for destroying (2 Cor. 10:8). (*The Second Helvetic Confession*, 18)

1. We are indebted in this chapter to the thoughts expressed by Frederica Mathewes-Green in "Church Discipline and the Post-Abortion Woman," Mark Ross in "Abortion and Church Discipline," and Gary LeTourneau in "Abortion and Church Discipline: A Response." All were unpublished papers presented at the Consultation on the Church and Abortion, Princeton, 1992.

One writer has compared church discipline to a root canal.[2] Its practice has all but disappeared from the church's life. In a culture where autonomy is exalted, church discipline is viewed by many as anachronistic and a violation of individual rights. If all opinions are valid, then it seems almost irrational to suggest that abortion, for example, constitutes an occasion for church discipline.

> If all opinions have equal authority and what I do is my concern and not someone else's, there is no longer any place for church discipline. No wonder it is no longer much used . . . because commonly accepted assumptions no longer undergird us.[3]

Church discipline may not seem to be conducive to church growth, either, particularly in those mainline denominations already suffering from declining membership. Our mobile society has developed something of a "club mentality" about church membership. People join and "unjoin" churches easily, not only when they move, but also when they decide that their needs are no longer being met. The customer, so to speak, is always right. Church membership vows set forth standards of accountability, but churches often are not inclined to press the matter, and many pastors question whether members would tolerate attempts to hold them accountable.

Churches shy away from discipline because the word itself, conjuring up images like that of Hester Prynne in Nathaniel Hawthorne's *Scarlet Letter*, seems to imply punishment and humiliation in situations that call instead for understanding and love.

Many pastors hope for the regenerative work of the Holy Spirit to produce changed lives without the necessity of church discipline. However, discipline is one means God has provided for the regenerative and restorative work of his Spirit. John Calvin said of it:

> . . . as the saving doctrine of Christ is the soul of the church, so does discipline serve as its sinews, through which the members of the body hold together, each in its own place. Therefore, all who desire to remove discipline or to hinder its restoration — whether they do

2. Tom Price, "Church Discipline and Reconciliation," *The Christian Century* (July 29-August 5, 1992), pp. 702-703.
3. Walter Cloisonne, as quoted by Tom Price; ibid., p. 702.

this deliberately or out of ignorance — are surely contributing to the ultimate dissolution of the church.[4]

## Discipline's Goal is Discipleship

Discipline is regarded as a mark of the church in some traditions. In others, it is an integral part of and implied by the sacrament of the Lord's Supper. As Calvin taught, church discipline has to do with guiding the congregation in the manner of life consistent with its affirmation of faith; it follows naturally from the preaching and hearing of the Word and from partaking of the sacraments. Therefore, church discipline is not first of all punitive. Rather, its primary purpose is training in discipleship. Just as athletes must train in order to compete successfully (cf. 1 Cor. 9:25), so discipleship requires well-disciplined physical and spiritual lives, and the objective of discipline in the church is a unified body, pleasing to God and productive for the kingdom.

The church exercises discipline in order to protect its people from sin and to preserve sound doctrine within its borders. There are many "winds of doctrine" abroad in our land these days, and church members are often "tossed to and fro" by them, "by people's trickery, by their craftiness in deceitful scheming" (Eph. 4:14 NRSV). Calvin, in a commentary on Matthew 25, compared false teachers in the church to wolves who trick God's flock to "rush of their own accord into the wolves' jaws, unless the shepherd whose heart is set on [the flock's] safety drives them off with shouts."[5] Church discipline preserves the Body of Christ as it preserves the message the body is charged to proclaim.

Discipline is also the means of reclaiming those who fall away. Jesus' parable of the lost sheep in Luke 15 expresses the benefits of discipline, not only to the erring, but also to the whole body, and to the Kingdom of God.

> Which one of you, having a hundred sheep and losing one of them, does not leave the ninety-nine in the wilderness and go after the

---

4. *Institutes of the Christian Religion* 4.12.1.

5. John Calvin, *New Testament Commentaries,* ed. David W. Torrance and Thomas F. Torrance (Grand Rapids: Wm. B. Eerdmans Publishing Co., 1989), 3.52.

one that is lost until he finds it? When he has found it, he lays it on his shoulders and rejoices. And when he comes home, he calls together his friends and neighbors, saying to them, "Rejoice with me, for I have found my sheep that was lost." Just so, I tell you, there will be more joy in heaven over one sinner who repents than over ninety-nine righteous persons who need no repentance. (vv. 4-7 NRSV)

Whenever an erring member is restored, the church itself is purified, and all the host of heaven rejoices.

Church discipline preserves the unity of the body. The church is meant to be a fellowship of believers, joined together in Christ by their hearing and believing of the Word, the vows they take as they receive the sacraments, and their common confession of faith. They are a people meant to know one another, to commune together, and to bear one another's burdens.

Fellowship and discipline are interdependent aspects of the church's life. Just as discipline depends on an existing body unified in the Word and sacraments and undergirded by a common faith, so also true fellowship among believers depends upon the exercise of discipline — persons accountable to one another, as well as to God, for how they are living their lives. It is discipline that makes baptism effective by training believers to bring their lives into conformity with the vows they take. It is discipline that offers protection to believers so that they can avoid partaking of the Lord's Table unworthily. Churches which strive to develop intimate fellowship among their members while avoiding discipline typically produce groups of people with no serious commitment to each other — people who enjoy superficial fellowship indistinguishable from the informal association of a club.

To be sure, there are perils on all sides in administering discipline in the church. Congregations have erred in making up their own lists of sins that have no basis in Scripture, or in failing to follow Scripture's requirement of evidence and confidentiality; they have been guilty of pettiness, of false accusations and gossip. But in our time, the more common error is neglect of the duty to discipline. The tendency of modern churches is to imitate the culture in providing therapy to cover over guilt, rather than in leading sinners to repentance, cleansing, and the blessing of restored lives. Churches that avoid discipline cannot help but trade God's power in Christ to transform lives for mere methods of coping. But it is because God's condemnation and judgment are real that the church is called both to issue warning in the hope of preventing members of the body from falling, and to declare the means of escape so that those who fall may be restored.

To the church alone God has entrusted the means of grace: true healing and true restoration for true guilt. Here is the key to abundant life: repentant lives and forgiven, cleansed consciences.

> My little children, I am writing these things to you so that you may not sin. But if anyone does sin, we have an advocate with the Father, Jesus Christ the righteous; and he is the atoning sacrifice for our sins, and not for ours only but also for the sins of the whole world. (1 John 2:1-2 NRSV)

The New Testament author of Hebrews writes, "For the moment all discipline seems painful rather than pleasant; later it yields the peaceful fruit of righteousness to those who have been trained by it" (Heb. 12:11). Practice of church discipline is meant to free those taken captive by sin. And it is meant to build up believers by helping them maintain cleansed consciences before God, and to aid them to live lives of holiness, so that those who are accustomed only to a diet of spiritual milk may grow into mature Christians (cf. Heb. 5:12-14).

## God's Action the Prelude to Repentance

The miracle of God's grace is that before we seek him — while we are yet in rebellion — "Christ died for us" (Rom. 5:8). He provided escape from our sins and death before we knew we needed it. That, the Bible tells us, is the Good News. That, said C. S. Lewis, is the joy that surprises us. God, by dying, overcomes death. Nihilism, which is the inevitable result of a universe without God, is overcome by the death and resurrection of Jesus Christ: that is the center of Christian faith. Because of what God did in Christ, an individual, in turning from sin, claims that grace, and lays hold of God's good intention for us. Repentance restores order to a universe made chaotic by sin.

God's mercy in the face of our rebellion is the model for the

95

church's behavior toward the sinner. While sin is an affront to God, God is not waiting to catch us doing wrong so that he can demand to be appeased. He knows us through and through, and has already made a way for us to be forgiven and restored to new life. Our repentance lets us lay hold of the miracle of grace that so transforms us that the past is finished and gone; all becomes new (2 Cor. 5:17).

## Now No Condemnation

Church discipline can err by so focusing on the condemnation of sin that it neglects the unconditional grace that no sin can render ineffectual.

> In Christ God has made fallen humanity his own. Faced with the fall, God did not step angrily aside. Instead he has personally united himself with the race. Lost humanity has been called home. . . . [Preaching] can be undertaken only in the knowledge that God himself has put everything right. . . . All that was required has actually been done to meet all human need. . . . Preachers are constantly tempted to proclaim human sins instead of this event, instead of God's goodness. . . . Now certainly something has to be said about human sins and errors. Yet it ought to be said from the standpoint of sin forgiven and error removed.[6]

On the other hand, Christ's death is the evidence of how serious a matter sin is to God. Shepherds of God imperil their flocks with teaching and preaching that avoids mention of sin, in particular those sins which church members themselves hope to rationalize. The traditional order of the church's worship calls Christians to confession and repentance, and always follows that by declaring the grace that was there before the confession was made: "In Jesus Christ, your sins are forgiven." But sin kept generalized — never specifically applied to the experience of church members — permits only the sort of peace that comes from a hardened conscience.

6. Karl Barth, *Homiletics* (Louisville: Westminster/John Knox Press, 1991), pp. 51-52.

# Applying Church Discipline to Abortion

The sin of abortion may be the most challenging opportunity in the church today for applying discipline. It is easy to avoid it by concluding that the risks are too great, the issue too divisive, and the pastor too vulnerable. One pastor, reflecting on the consequences of avoiding the risks, wrote:

> There are four losers . . . : the unborn babies, who continue to die even at the hands of their Christian mothers; the mothers, who are never warned prior to their sin and never have the opportunity to repent and be restored following an abortion; the church, which experiences the pollution of repeated and unconfessed sin by its members; and last, but not least, the minister, who certainly feels guilty, and who is guilty of the sin of silence in the face of the slaughter of innocent victims.[7]

An Episcopalian priest testified to the effect of the church's unwillingness to aid in restoring those who bear the guilt of abortion. The priest gave passive assent to his wife's abortion and was burdened with guilt because he knew that canon law prohibits the ordination of anyone who has "positively cooperated" in the procurement of an abortion.[8] He also knew that 1 Timothy 3 calls for morally exemplary leadership in the church. Yet, he could not turn to his own bishop for spiritual help "because I doubted his ability to speak with authority to me, given his own pro-choice position." In his misery, he turned to the Roman Catholic archbishop of his city who, he later testified, "gave me back the soul I had lost."

People of good heart and generous spirit frequently try to encourage those who have been through an abortion with well-meaning assurances that there were mitigating circumstances. But their efforts do not bring the peace of God. Anesthesia may relieve the pain temporarily, but it does not cure the illness or restore the body.

When the church proclaims the sin of abortion it warns some of God's flock away from wrongdoing, and aids the confession of others who need to take their first step of response to God's forgiving grace.

7. Gary LeTourneau, *Response*, p. 3.
8. Roman Catholic *Code of Canon Law*, 1041.

97

If, instead, the church is silent or tries to find justification for abortion, it inadvertently refuses the opportunity for confession and thus closes the door to forgiveness. It encourages those living with the guilt of abortion to harden their hearts. It is the role of the church to provide the means by which men and women may find their way back to God, "whether they hear or refuse to hear" (cf. Ezek. 3).

## Leaders as Models

How, then, can the church prepare to exercise discipline in the matter of abortion so that the body is edified and sinful lives restored to wholeness?

First, the complicity of the church itself must be taken into account. Churches that have generally neglected the practice of discipline must first establish a basis for accountability. They will need to plan conscientiously to build discipline into all areas of the lives of their communities. Pastors and church leaders might well begin with their own self-examination that precedes partaking of the Lord's Supper. They should have opportunity for confession and repentance and for yielding themselves voluntarily in mutual submission and accountability. The model of godliness in the lives of the church's leaders bears witness to the congregation and to the community at large and is strong preventive medicine (cf. 1 Pet. 2:11, 12).

Church leaders should spend time together studying the documents that will teach them the right exercise of church discipline: Scripture, the confessions, and the disciplinary documents of their own tradition. In that way those who bear leadership responsibility in the church will be instructed both in the goals and the proper steps of discipline and begin to practice it in every area of the church's life. All members of the body ought to receive instruction in church discipline since all bear responsibility for the care and spiritual accountability of fellow members.

## Preaching and Teaching as Discipline

The exercise of discipline in the congregation begins with the right preaching of the Word and its application to all areas of Christian life. The first hope in the disciplinary life of the church is to protect God's people from falling. Attention to the preaching and teaching ministries of the church will begin to enliven the consciences of the people of God and equip them to avoid occasions for sin.

The ordinary life of the church is filled with opportunities for the exercise of discipline. For example, one youth group leader told of his first experience in teaching biblical views of sexual relationships. One surprised young woman interrupted him and said, "Wait a minute. I know that the Bible teaches me to be faithful to my husband when I get married, but are you telling me that sexual relationships before marriage are wrong?" The youth leader found himself suddenly in a situation that called for clear and gentle admonition. And, in fact, his entire effort to convey biblical teaching about sexual relationships was disciplinary because of his hope to protect those young people and to produce repentant amendment of life where necessary.

Children and youth today are subject to teaching and influences in the culture that encourage sexual activity as a normal part of growing up, as an aspect of self-discovery. In many communities contraception and abortion are readily available to help young people avoid "problem" pregnancies. The church that hopes for its children to grow in the nurture and admonition of the Lord will provide instruction on God's intent in sexual relationships, in marriage and the formation of family, and in living single lives that honor God.

A teenage girl, testifying before a denomination committee studying abortion, pleaded for help from the church to counter the messages from the society. "Teach us," she said:

> Teach us to pattern our lives after [our Lord]. Show us the error of living for ourselves. . . . Instill in us a reverence and awe for God's power. Reaffirm his creation of the entire world and all that is in it. Teach us that we were fearfully and wonderfully made, each one with a specific plan, designed for use by God himself. Help us to feel special because of who we are and to feel fulfilled in living the lives Christ called us to live.

But she also pleaded for the church's help when teens fall prey to the culture's lure.

> Be there for us when one of us becomes pregnant through tragic circumstances or stumbles and does not follow God's plan of purity for our lives. When we have sinned, we need people who will lovingly draw us to seek our own forgiveness. Don't let us go to church and find that it sanctions a procedure which kills [the unborn]. We need the church to teach us the emotional, moral, and physical dangers of abortion. . . . We want the church to follow Jesus' example of not only providing spiritual teaching but also meeting physical needs. Jesus said in Matt. 25:40, "I tell you the truth, whatever you did for one of the least of these brothers of mine, you did for me."[9]

## Leading Gently to Repentance

The preaching and teaching ministry of the church ought to be sufficient in most cases to draw out whatever confessions need to be made. The church ought to guard itself against a suspicious search for sin among its members. That would be an abuse of its disciplinary responsibility.

Matthew 18:15-20 sets forth an approach to correction of an erring brother or sister that protects him or her as much as possible both from public humiliation, and from becoming a subject of gossip.

Following the guidance of that passage, church discipline related to abortion — just as to any other sin — should be handled, as much as possible, privately and with complete confidentiality. The spirit of the discipline ought to be conducive to repentance prompted by the possibility of forgiveness and restoration. As 2 Timothy 2:24-26 states, we as the Lord's servants must not be quarrelsome but kindly to everyone, apt teachers, patient, correcting [even] opponents with gentleness, in the hopes that they will "repent and come to know the truth."

However, Matthew 18:16 teaches that when the offending party refuses to listen to the admonition of a brother or sister, witnesses

9. Testimony by Dorothy DeCamp to the Special Committee on Problem Pregnancies and Abortion was reprinted in the *Presbyterians Pro-Life News* (Minneapolis, Fall-Winter, 1990-1991), p. 8.

ought to be brought in. In these cases it may be helpful to bring a witness who not only knows about the abortion, but also can give testimony of her own restored life. The church should never initiate action toward a woman on the basis of a secondhand report of her abortion, except at the request of the family of a minor child who has undergone the procedure.

The exercise of discipline may find its occasion quite incidentally. For example, the church may discover that one of its members is an abortionist. Or a church member may openly advocate for abortion or aid in its procurement. On the other hand, a man or woman, hearing the message of Scripture applied to abortion, may quietly seek out a pastor or other trusted church member in order to make confession.

Some women confess their sin in contrition, while others demonstrate hardened or deadened consciences in defending their decisions. The church should approach every woman with gentleness, extending to her the forgiveness available in Christ, as well as the hope of complete restoration to fellowship with God and with the church, and of new and obedient, joyful life in Christ.

Especially given the widespread sanction of abortion in our society and in some quarters of the church, discipline of a woman who has had an abortion should not go beyond private admonition unless the woman herself makes it public. If she spurns the help of the one to whom she has made confession, the proper recourse is to pray for her, and not to neglect any opportunity to lead her further toward repentance. She may eventually seek out help if those who counsel her keep in mind that they do not want to close off any possibility of her spiritual restoration. Sometimes those who defend abortion are in fact rationalizing their own decision or their encouragment of someone else's decision to have one.

The church should explain to those who persist in a hardened practice of any sin — repeatedly performing or abetting abortions, or engaging in profligate sexual practices, for example — in spite of warnings and opportunities to repent, that they have repudiated the vows they made to God and to the body and have separated themselves from their Lord and the church. This action is a last resort, but sometimes finally necessary and, in those cases, the objective continues always to be the repentance and restoration of the sinner.

Scripture instructs us that those who hold office in the church ought to be models in faith and behavior that God's people can be encouraged to follow. The Scripture also teaches that we all sin and fall short of God's glory; it is persistence in sin, refusal to repent, or calling good what Scripture calls evil that would call not only for disciplinary action but for barring a member from holding office in the church or requiring removal from office.[10]

One feature of discipline that distinguishes it from purely punitive action is the emphasis on restoration. One Presbyterian pastor testified to the blessing of church discipline. His youngest daughter became pregnant as an unmarried high school student. After confessing both her pregnancy and the sexual sin to her parents, she agreed to make confession also to the church elders and to put herself under their disciplinary care. Although the elders were unaccustomed to bearing that sort of responsibility, they took the young woman under their wing and promised to help her keep her promise of repentance to God. The young woman was so obviously the object of love and care by church leaders that eventually the young man, who at first had shunned the girl, came forward to confess and to put himself under their care as well.

The church can encourage faithfulness by acknowledging the enticement of sin that is particularly prevalent in our culture, and encouraging members in the private and public habits that protect them from temptation. The church can provide well-chaperoned group activities for its teenagers, and opportunities for adult fellowship for those both single and married. And the church can affirm the wholeness and abundance of life in Jesus Christ that can fulfill human beings whether they live as chaste singles or as those whose sexual lives are expressed in marriage.

The very real temptations to immorality in our world make this an important area for loving and encouraging accountability in the church.

---

10. In recent decades this stricture is exemplified in the refusal by many denominations to ordain self-affirming, practicing, *unrepentant* homosexuals. It should not be considered extraordinary, therefore, for the church to exercise the same discipline toward those who persist in other sexually profligate behavior or in abortion.

# The Involvement of Others

Abortion is nearly always the result of sexual sin; churches that begin to restore discipline to the body may be surprised by the incidence of sexual sin in their midst. Abortion always involves more than the mother acting alone. In every case there is also a father who has responsibility, whether he knows it or not, for the safety and well-being of the child. The church's help in restoring the lives of its people who are guilty of sexual sin is important whether or not abortion is involved. And the church's attention to sexual sin may avert abortion altogether in some cases, and prevent further abortions in others.

Family members and friends of the woman may share her culpability because of their failure even to attempt to dissuade or help her, or because they encouraged or even coerced her to have the abortion. Grandparents or fathers may be living with a silent knowledge of the part they played in an abortion. Professional counselors, including pastors and medical personnel, all bear responsibility if they have advised abortion. Discipline will be most effective if it can be administered to all the parties involved in the abortion, enabling them to be reconciled to each other as well as to God and the body of believers, and supportive of each other in attempts to "henceforth live lives pleasing to God."

The church must guard itself against regarding the woman involved in abortion as a victim. Even if she was pressured to have the abortion by a boyfriend, her family, or her friends, she is responsible for her own decision. It is dehumanizing to regard a woman as if she were not responsible for her actions. If the church puts the responsibility elsewhere and ignores the woman's sin, it will leave her in captivity to what she knows she has done. The best help a woman can receive is the opportunity to confess and the assurance that she can be forgiven. Mother Teresa's well-known statement that there are two deaths in every abortion — the child and the conscience of the mother — expresses what is at stake in the church's relationship to the woman.

Church discipline acknowledges that there are truths worth preserving and souls worth rescuing. It demonstrates that the Word is not an opinion or one truth among many. It takes seriously the destructive effects of false teachings and of sin. Church discipline is an active assertion that we are not alone in the universe, but rather that we belong to God and are always accountable to him.

# CHAPTER 8

# *Abortion and the Church's Ministry of Service*

The ministry of the church to others is service to God, a response to grace, done in obedience to the will of God made known in Scripture.[1]

In the last analysis, the Christian church is a missionary body. It has a mission "to declare the wonderful deeds of him who called [it] out of darkness into his marvelous light" (1 Pet. 2:9). It is sent into the world to make disciples of all persons, by telling them what God has done for them through Jesus Christ, by drawing all persons into its fellowship through baptism, and by teaching them to live according to God's will revealed in Jesus Christ (Matt. 28:19-20). It desires, in the love of Christ, that all people everywhere may know his forgiveness, his redemption, his righteousness, his sanctification, his wisdom (1 Cor. 1:30), and his promise of eternal and joyful life in his kingdom that is coming.

The church can make a difference in the lives of individuals by believing its own message: not only by proclaiming the message truthfully and with conviction, but also by living out that message in its own life.

The book of James contains an argument about faith. Shall we

---

1. "Directory for the Service of God," *The Constitution of the Presbyterian Church (U.S.A.), Part II, Book of Order 1983-85* (New York and Atlanta: Office of the General Assembly of the Presbyterian Church [U.S.A.], 1983), S-2.0400, para. 1.

say that faith is believing only, it asks, or shall we not rather see that faith is confirmed and made visible by our actions. Worship is *leiturgia*, "work" for the Lord, and finally God's work involves the world, which he loves (John 3:16). God wants all persons everywhere "to glorify him and enjoy him forever." The church must render practical service with the hands and feet of the people in her community which will ensure and nurture the life that God has created and which will raise that life to Christian maturity. Scripture admonishes us to be doers of the Word, and not hearers only (Jas. 1:22).

There are thousands of women who have had abortions because they thought they had no alternative. One said, "If I'd known someone was there to help me, I would *never* have had an abortion."[2] John Cardinal O'Connor, who promises help from the Roman Catholic church to any woman who seeks it, reports surveys in which the majority of women echo that refrain. They say they chose abortion because no one told them help was available.

## God Equips the Church for Service

God equips his church to respond to human needs. The nature of the church's new community in the Spirit, its broad reach geographically, its makeup of people, and its mission, ideally suit the church to respond in very practical ways to the needs presented in a crisis pregnancy.

The nature of the church's community equips it to serve. It is the communion of the saints embodied concretely within the local church — that fellowship of people who know each other and share one another's lives and care for each other — which constitutes its great potential gift to pregnant women and their families and their children, born and unborn. In that community not only is the gospel preached, with its words of forgiveness and restoration, but persons are adopted into the family of God by baptism and made members of the body of Christ. In that local fellowship, the new life in Christ is repeatedly

2. Quoted by Carol Risser, in her paper presented to the Princeton Consultation on The Church and Abortion, "An Action Agenda for Pro-Life Congregations" (1991), p. 2.

offered in the Lord's Supper, and church members are united together in peace in communion with their God and one another. In that setting, every unwed mother can be welcomed and supported, and the birth of every child can be celebrated. In that special community, all children can be raised up "in the nurture and admonition of the Lord" (Eph. 6:4 KJV). In that communion of forgiven sinners, new patterns of sexual and family life can be learned. The commitment of Christians to live out the love of Christ for his world can be very specific in the local church. C. Everett Koop, speaking particularly in response to crisis pregnancies, pointed out that

> . . . before we had government programs it was the Christian church that saw to the care of the sick, the disadvantaged, the poor, the underprivileged, and so on. I believe the Christian church must retrieve that role, which it served so well in the past. Churches and individual Christians can do the job far better than it can be done from Washington, and they can do it in a way that witnesses to Christian love.[3]

We in the church must not presume to counsel courage to women in crisis pregnancies without being willing ourselves, as Christ's body, to share in the bearing of their burdens. It is we who must hear and heed the admonition to faithfulness first, and offer not only the spiritual help that so much of this book addresses, but also the tangible help that will encourage and sustain those women in crisis.

> If a brother or sister is ill-clad and in lack of daily food, and one of you says to them, "Go in peace, be warmed and filled," without giving them the things needed for the body, what does it profit? (Jas. 2:15-17)

The church can prepare itself consciously to be the community into which a woman and child are welcomed and cared for in the long-term. The church can play a significant role in ending the crisis and can be the place where mother and child *belong* long after the crisis has passed.

3. "Problem-Pregnancy Help: The Church Must do More," *Pastoral Renewal* (April 1985), p. 141.

The scattered location of churches equips them for service. Churches are located in communities beyond the reach of social service agencies. There are few places where people live that the Christian church has not found them and been established among them, from densely populated cities to remote rural areas, from among the very rich to the poorest of the poor.

God's own provisions supply the church to meet the needs of others, in material goods and in talents and professional skills, and in the fruits of love he brings to bear in his people, that lead them to offer generous service. As the account of the church in 2 Corinthians 9 shows, not every individual church is ready at all times to meet every need, but the connected body of Christ can ensure that nothing is lacking.

> And God is able to provide you with every blessing in abundance, so that by always having enough of everything, you may share abundantly in every good work. (2 Cor. 9:8 NRSV)

What are the tangible needs in a crisis pregnancy? Medical care? A place to live? Food and clothing? Child care? Education? A job? Family? Legal assistance? Adoption? Which of these needs exceeds the church's ability to help? Churches can provide financial assistance, food and housing, maternity and infant clothing and baby showers, as well as baby-sitting services and day-care centers, budgeting and other economic guidance, education in child rearing or tutoring help for child or parent, vocational guidance and help in finding employment, medical and other emergency care. The list is almost as endless as Christian concern, creativity, and imagination.

Even very poor churches can provide a wealth of help to women in crisis. Older women can teach younger women the skills they learned in raising their own children. Even the most unskilled lay person with a big heart can provide love and concern and companionship, just as the most elderly and infirm in a congregation can carry on the ministry of daily prayer, undergirding the efforts of others. God promises to bless the offering of even the smallest gift.

> He looked up and saw rich people putting their gifts into the treasury; he also saw a poor widow put in two small copper coins. He said, "Truly I tell you, this poor widow has put in more than all of

them; for all of them have contributed out of their abundance, but she out of her poverty has put in all she had to live on." (Luke 21:1-4 NRSV)

Jesus promised to care for our material needs (Matt. 6:25-34). The miraculous provision of food in both Old and New Testaments shows God's intent to care for the basic needs of life for his people. The biblical admonition to share both out of our abundance and when our own resources seem insufficient[4] is opportunity for those in the church to demonstrate that they believe and trust God. By unstinting care for women and their unborn children the church can testify to the world that there are no unwanted children. This loving, life-preserving service is entirely in keeping with the mission of the church.

## Not a Welfare System

In its service, the church functions much more like a family than a community social service agency. It provides the care and accountability of a family, especially if the woman's own family relationships are otherwise broken. It is the church's business to help reconcile broken relationships. The church provides help, not after the model of a welfare system, but of the kind undertaken by family members, help that avoids long-term dependency. The church cares little about rights and entitlements and a great deal about spiritual relationships and growth in discipleship. The church is able not only to care for the protection of children in the womb, but also for children as they grow to adulthood. The church is interested not only in seeing an immediate crisis resolved, but also in building character with eternity in mind.

The Christian gospel is quite clear that we are all responsible before God for the use of our lives. Those aided by the church, therefore, should be helped in such a way that they develop responsible strategies before God for their actions, their employment, their children, and their family lives. The church should extend aid where help is needed, but the final goal is nurture of the needy that enables them to become mature Christians, able then to help others.

4. Consider, for example, the story of Elijah and the widow of Zarephath in 1 Kings 17.

The church's objective in a crisis pregnancy is to consider both the means of preserving the life and well-being of the unborn child, and the long-term well-being of the pregnant woman. Preserving the life of the child means not only avoiding abortion but also planning for the future of the child in a stable family and supportive community. Caring for the well-being of the pregnant woman means consideration of medical care for her and her child, as well as her economic, emotional, social, and spiritual needs.

Each church needs a plan in place so that when a crisis situation is presented, both the immediate and long-term needs can be met. In communities where there are pregnancy care centers, churches have a ready resource for help over the hump of the immediate crisis. In areas where no community center exists, it will be important for the church to plan how it will go about providing for a pregnant woman's emergency needs.

The church also needs a long-term plan to ensure that it is equipped as a community to live in relationship with the mother and child. Primarily it is a plan for helping a woman in crisis establish a stable life for herself and her child with the loving support of the community of believers.

## Meeting the Immediate Needs in a Crisis

When abortion became legal in the United States by the action of the Supreme Court, the incidence grew to enormous proportions very quickly. From fewer than 20,000 abortions in the late 1960s, the numbers rapidly increased to over 600,000 in 1973 and then soared to a reported 1,600,000 yearly in recent years. The United States has one of the highest abortion rates among developed countries.[5]

One of the first responses to the legalization of abortion was an increase in abortion services. But another response was the emergence of abortion-alternative services — very often organized by

5. The early figures are taken from Christopher Tietze and Stanley K. Henshaw, *Induced Abortion, A World Review* (New York: The Alan Guttmacher Institute, 1986), p. 41. The current figure appears in "Facts in Brief," published by the Alan Guttmacher Institute, New York, 1993.

Christian women — aimed to counsel, befriend, and care for women in crisis pregnancies, with the hope of helping those women and preserving the lives of their children. The number of these services has grown to equal or exceed the number of abortion providers.

Typically abortion-alternative organizations are supported financially by churches and individuals, and the services often are delivered by trained volunteers; many of the volunteers themselves have degrees and certifications in areas related to the services they provide.

While the services vary widely, they may include counseling regarding the woman's decisions in the crisis, the effects of an abortion, sexual practices that led to an unexpected pregnancy, and the woman's needs in preparation for motherhood. Some provide "shepherding" families — or group homes with houseparents — where women may live during pregnancy and for a time after delivery; job counseling and training; education; pre- and post-natal medical services as well as delivery of babies; maternity and baby clothing and other items for the baby; and adoption services. In many cases these community organizations exemplify the body of Christ standing against a great moral evil by bending down to serve. Because many of these services have a distinctly Christian mission, the women they serve may not only change their minds about needing abortions, but also find new life in Jesus Christ.

Many churches already involved in helping women are acquainted with pregnancy care services in their communities and have developed working relationships with them. Some churches maintain a comprehensive list of available referral sources in their communities.

The strength of these community services is that they exist to meet and resolve a crisis, and the relationships they develop with women may be intense for a period of several weeks. They serve women both inside and outside the church. These community-based centers serve as an important restraint against abortion, and are, in a sense, a rebuke to the church's neglect of the moral, spiritual and material needs that have led so many women to choose abortion. Their work is worthy of the church's support.

## Options for Raising the Child

Perhaps the most important practical help the church can provide is counsel and encouragement as the woman considers the options of future family life for herself and her unborn baby. Her alternatives are marriage, adoption, and single parenting, nearly always by the mother, sometimes with the help of her parents or extended family. In each case the objective of the church is to increase the long-term prospects for both mother and child for a stable family life.

## The Option of Marriage

In the 1950s, fear of social ostracism and lack of institutional and financial support, as well as moral influences, served as restraints on the impulses of teenagers to become sexually active before marrying[6]; only five percent of the nation's births were out of wedlock.[7] Fewer than one out of ten unmarried pregnant women who gave birth chose single-parenthood, and some of those single mothers soon married because there was already a commitment on the part of the father. In cases where the young man was unwilling to take responsibility, or the young woman or the parents involved decided that marriage would not be a good option at that point, typically the young woman would continue her pregnancy away from home and plan for the baby's adoption.

By the 1980s nearly a million teenagers were becoming pregnant each year, and about half were keeping their babies. By the 1990s nearly one in every four children was born out of wedlock.[8] Standards of sexual morality had changed dramatically in the intervening decades; the stigma associated with unwed pregnancy was significantly diminished; and both assistance programs and counseling of young women began to favor single parenthood.[9]

6. Susan Olasky and Marvin Olasky, *More Than Kindness: A Compassionate Approach to Crisis Childbearing* (Wheaton, Illinois: Crossway Books, 1990), pp. 22-24.

7. Barbara Dafoe Whitehead, "Dan Quayle Was Right," *The Atlantic Monthly* (April 1993), p. 48.

8. Ibid., p. 50.

9. *Olasky and Olasky, More Than Kindness*, pp. 25-28.

The results have been disastrous not only for individuals and their babies, but also for the whole of society. *The Atlantic Monthly*, in April of 1993, published an article on out-of-wedlock births, at a historic high in 1992, which concluded that,

> . . . family diversity in the form of increasing numbers of single-parent and stepparent families does not strengthen the social fabric but, rather, dramatically weakens and undermines society.[10]

Among its litany of negative findings in comparing children of single parent homes to those with two parents were that children in single parent homes are six times more likely to be poor, two to three times more likely to have emotional and behavioral problems, more likely to drop out of high school, to get pregnant as teenagers, to abuse drugs, to have run-ins with the law, and to be physically or sexually abused. In the last two decades teen suicide has more than tripled, juvenile crime has increased and become more violent, and school performance has declined.[11]

Some single parents do a marvelous and courageous job of raising their children. However, the sociological data does not favor single parenthood as either the best situation in which to bring up children or as the best of alternatives to abortion. The biblical model of father and mother fares much better overall.

While it may not always be possible to avoid both single parenthood and abortion, churches can shape their influences on young men and women to discourage sexual promiscuity and, where pregnancies occur, discourage the two most damaging options: abortion and single parenthood. We do not need the results of sociological research to know that both marriage and adoption have better prospects for providing a stable home life for parents and children. But the disaster of single parenthood — and its increasing likelihood in our modern sexually promiscuous environment — is added incentive for the church to lift up high standards for relationships between young men and women that emphasize restraint, and the blessing of sexual relationships within the bonds of marriage. Those standards are communicated both in the preaching and teaching ministry of the

10. Whitehead, "Quayle," p. 47.
11. Ibid., pp. 47-48.

113

church and, just as importantly, in the witness of the lives of families in the church who choose to live in obedient response to God's Word and counter to the prevailing views about sexuality and marriage in the culture.

Common wisdom assumes that teenage marriages are dis-astrous, but that is not necessarily the case. Surveys have shown that a significant number of teen marriages involving a pregnancy have become stable families. Both father and mother may mature rapidly in assuming the responsibility of parenthood. Unmarried fathers often discover they have a strong interest in the child they helped conceive, and many are willing, particularly with encouragement and help, to assume long-term responsibility for the upbringing of their children.[12]

## Remember the Fathers

The sexual mores of our modern culture discourage expectations that unmarried fathers will assume responsibility for their children, and encourage the expectation that the responsibility of young men to their children is no more than the cost of an abortion if the mother chooses that route, or of complete desertion is she does not. The church can restrain such low standards of behavior in young men by reaffirming God's intent for sexual relationships, for the forming of families, and the long-term commitments involved. In its preaching and teaching and in the mores of its own community life, the church can lift up the high calling of fatherhood.

> [God] established a testimony in Jacob,
> and appointed a law in Israel,
> which he commanded our fathers
> to teach to their children;
> that the next generation might know them,
> the children yet unborn,

12. See Olasky and Olasky, "Supporting the Two-Parent Family," in *More Than Kindness*, pp. 137-153, for a discussion of the results of a number of studies of teen marriages. The Olaskys are to be credited with suggesting, for what may be the first time in several decades, that the possibility of marriage ought to be mentioned in a crisis pregnancy.

and arise and tell them to their children,
so that they should set their hope in God. . . .

(Ps. 78:5-7)

The apostle writes that fathers should bring up their children in the discipline and instruction of the Lord (Eph. 6:4). Gilbert Milaender notes this biblical instruction and says, "In many respects this is the most fundamental task of parents: transmission of a way of life."[13] It is a high calling for fathers as well as for mothers, and one that can reorient the lives of young parents who may have viewed sexuality as completely detached from family responsibility prior to the advent of a child.

The community of believers can make a significant contribution to breaking the cycle of poverty, violence, family breakdown, and sexual promiscuity that is often the result of men abandoning their obligations for the children they father.

We in the church ought always to regard marriage as an option to be explored in a crisis pregnancy. We should not assume that a young mother is too immature to marry but mature enough for single motherhood.

## The Option of Adoption

Moses' mother saved his life, first by attempting to hide him when his life was threatened, and then by cooperating in his adoption:

> And when he was abandoned, Pharaoh's daughter adopted him, and brought him up as her own son. (Acts 7:21 NRSV)

Certainly not without the pain of loss, adoption was nonetheless a life-saving alternative for Moses. His story shows us how carefully God arranged the circumstances of his young life, not only to rescue him from almost certain death, but also to prepare him for the calling God gave him. Human adoption is something of a living metaphor for a strong biblical theme of what God did for us in Jesus Christ. The gospel

---

13. "The Meaning of the Presence of Children," an unpublished paper (1993), pp. 8-9.

message carries a strong affirmation of each believer's spiritual adoption. Adoption expresses our transformation from condemnation to grace, from our utter rejection to our complete acceptance. And it is acceptance based on no merit of our own, but on the fact that God loves us and wants us:

> . . . you have received a spirit of adoption. When we cry, "Abba, Father!" it is that very Spirit bearing witness with our spirit that we are children of God, and if children, then heirs, heirs of God and joint heirs with Christ. . . . (Rom. 8:15b-18 NRSV)

Adoption is a legitimate avenue for providing a child with a stable home where the child of a crisis situation is truly wanted. In most situations, the child is wanted by both birth mother and adoptive parents. The birth mother wants a permanent, stable home for her child and makes the sacrifices necessary to provide that; the adoptive parents make the daily sacrifices necessary to provide the permanence and stability important to the lifelong well-being of the child.

But adoption is seldom even offered as an option to women in crisis pregnancy situations, and it is the option least chosen by women in crisis pregnancies. Abortion and single parenthood are the two most frequently chosen options.

One lawyer and adoptive parent explained,

> If a pregnant teenager goes to one of the major adoption agencies in Minnesota, for example, and requests adoption counseling, her first counseling sessions consist of instructions on how to apply for AFDC, medical assistance and subsidized housing. The emphasis in the "counseling" sessions is instruction in all the ways a teenager can avail herself of governmental programs to facilitate her keeping the child, rather than placing the child for adoption.
>
> Not surprisingly, statistics from this particular agency indicate that 95 percent of the pregnant women who come to the agency contemplating adoption end up keeping their child. This statistic is consistent with national figures. . . .[14]

14. Corey L. Gordon, "Society Needs to Encourage Adoption," *The Minneapolis Tribune* (Oct. 6, 1990), p. 13A.

Olasky and Olasky found that social workers and counselors in general assume that pregnant adolescents have no interest in adoption. Studies show that, on the contrary, "despite almost universal verbal disapproval, some girls had in fact considered adoption, but the resultant community and familial pressures against it were so pervasive that they were unable to carry through with their plans."[15] Pregnant adolescents find little or no support in exploring adoption as an alternative to abortion.

The other side of this coin is that at least two million childless couples on waiting lists or in fertility clinics hope to adopt. They wait an average of four years for a healthy Caucasian infant, and even ten years is not unusual.[16] Often the prospective parents are considered too old to adopt by the time a child becomes available; and typically it is more difficult to adopt a second child than a first, because eligible couples without any children are given preference. The dearth of available children in recent decades has led an increasing number of couples to places all over the globe in search for children to adopt. The frustrating experiences of childless couples — and of couples willing to add special-needs children to their families — would fill a book of its own.

Approximately one-third of abortions each year are among teenagers. There are about thirty abortions for every adoption, though the number of prospective adoptive parents exceeds the number of aborted babies. Over half a million unmarried teenagers (most of them between the ages of 15-19) give birth each year, but fewer than ten percent of those babies are placed in adoptive homes. Ninety percent of those unmarried young women choose to keep their babies.[17] And three-fifths of all children born out-of-wedlock, and their mothers, are dependent on government welfare for subsistence.[18]

15. Judith S. Musick, Arden Handler, and Katherine Downs Waddill, "Teens and Adoption: A Pregnancy Resolution Alternative?" *Children Today* (November/December 1984), p. 28, quoted in Olasky and Olasky, *More Than Kindness*, p. 39.

16. Charlotte Low Allen, "Special Delivery: Overcoming the Barriers to Adoption," *Policy Review* (Washington, D.C.: The Heritage Foundation, Summer 1989), p. 46.

17. *Adoption Factbook: United States Data, Issues, Regulations and Resources*, published by the National Council For Adoption, Washington, D.C., June 1989, pp. 127-129.

18. Olasky and Olasky, *More Than Kindness*, p. 31.

Only about three-to-seven percent of *all* women of any age who give birth out-of-wedlock decide on adoption for their babies. Currently there are approximately 50,000 adoptions by non-relatives each year — including foreign adoptions — and another roughly 90,000 adoptions by relatives, including thousands still never formally adopted.[19] Adopted children include those with severe disabilities and some who are terminally ill. Many couples are waiting specifically to adopt children with conditions such as Down's Syndrome or spina bifida.[20]

The number of difficult-to-place children available for adoption is about 36,000, a relatively small number: they are beyond infancy, and members of racial minorities, or suffering from physical or mental disabilities. Another 240,000 children, victims of some form of abuse, languish in foster homes because their parents refuse to relinquish custody.[21] A recent federal study found 22,000 babies abandoned in urban hospitals.[22]

## Barriers to Adoption

Would-be adoptive parents greatly outnumber the children available, once abortion has taken its toll. Furthermore, if adoption laws and agency requirements were more reasonable, and the costs less prohibitive, we might expect an even larger number of couples to seek adoption.

Adoptions can range from no cost to well in excess of $15,000. A study of costs in 1986 showed that roughly a quarter of legal adoptions were done at no fee, but it is not uncommon to pay $5,000, or even well over $10,000, regardless of whether the child is adopted inside or outside the U.S.[23] The costs for adoption are often higher than for

19. Allen, "Special Delivery," p. 46-47.

20. "The Adoption Option," *The Wall Street Journal* (July 7, 1989), p. A6.

21. Allen, "Special Delivery," p. 48.

22. Barbara Vobejda, " 'A Big Warning Sign': 22,000 'Boarder Babies' in U.S.," *The Washington Post* (Nov. 10, 1993), pp. A1, 23. The federal study noted that nearly half of these babies are healthy. Because they have been abandoned, however, it can take years to place them in permanent homes.

23. *Adoption Factbook*, pp. 207-208.

natural childbirth. Further, childbirth is usually covered by health insurance plans, while adoption typically is not.

Health insurance can pose a serious barrier for couples seeking to adopt children from overseas or a child with existing health care needs. Some states still allow insurance companies to refuse health insurance coverage in those cases.

Policies and laws governing the adoption of African-American and Native American babies keep many of them out of stable homes and often in long-term foster care. Placement for African-American babies is a particular problem. The National Association of Black Social Workers has been at work since 1972 to end interracial adoptions and about 35 states currently ban them. By contrast, the state of Texas forbids discrimination in adoption. Two-thirds of difficult-to-place children are black and two-thirds of families waiting to adopt are white.[24] In spite of exhaustive studies showing the healthy development of children in interracial adoptions, and the willingness of prospective adoptive couples to choose them, thousands of African-American children remain in foster care.[25]

The Indian Child Welfare Act of 1978, instituted as an important protection of the sovereignty of tribal governments, has much the same result as do laws governing the placement of African-American babies. In 1986, for example, over 9000 Indian children were in substitute care, but only 340 were eligible for adoption.[26]

Other laws pertaining to open and cooperative adoptions are of questionable benefit to the well-being of the child. Mary Beth Style, from the National Council for Adoption in Washington, D.C., reported in 1994 that some trends in adoption are more like foster care placements because the adoptive parents are not sure that the placement will be permanent. Though the notion of maintaining the possibility of contact with the child may appeal to the birth mother as she considers adoption, only about one percent of adoptees ever search for their biological parents.[27]

24. Maria McFadden, "Rapping Adoption," *The Human Life Review* (New York, Summer 1993), p. 45.
25. *Adoption Factbook,* pp. 123-124. The chapter cites specific studies of the success of interracial adoptions.
26. Ibid., p. 183.
27. Allen, "Special Delivery," p. 52.

Perhaps the most significant barrier to adoption is the promotion in our society of an attitude that adoption is largely a negative experience for all concerned. Horror stories abound in the press, casting adoptive parents as troubled and abusive. Birth mothers are counseled that adoption is a painful "limbo loss" that lasts a lifetime, whereas abortion is final.[28] That counsel overlooks entirely the effects of abortion on a young woman. While the public is flooded with painful accounts of women whose children have been adopted, the firsthand accounts women give of their experiences with the profound effects of abortion, some physical and others psychological and spiritual, are rarely reported by the media. In one survey, 344 women who had had abortions reported feelings of guilt (66%), nightmares (22%), regret and remorse (54%), despair (27%), inability to forgive themselves (46%), and depression (57%). Seven percent had attempted suicide.[29] The stories these women have to tell offer perspective on the after-effects of adoption.

Adoptive children are often portrayed as having extraordinary problems. But comparisons are typically made to two-parent birth families, rather than to the single-parent families which is the actual option in this situation, and where the prospects for the future are grimmest of all. Additionally, the comparisons fail to consider the distinction between children adopted as babies and older children finally adopted after years of abuse or life in multiple foster homes. In contrast to many media portrayals, researchers find generally that adopted children do well. Most of them do well when compared to those born into two-parent families. They are certainly among the most wanted of children.[30]

28. McFadden, "Rapping Adoption," p. 41. She quotes the new version of *Our Bodies, Ourselves* (by The Boston Women's Health Book Collective, published in New York by Simon and Schuster): "The loss of a child to adoption is a unique and unnatural one. Unlike death, which is final, adoption creates a loss that is renewed daily. . . . It is a limbo loss." The obvious conclusion is that the mother is better off with a dead child than planning for that child's adoption by a barren couple.

29. "Physical and Psychological Injury in Women Following Abortion: Akron Pregnancy Services Survey," published in Washington, D.C. by the Association for Interdisciplinary Research in Values and Social Change, Sept/Oct. 1993, Vol. 5 No. 4, p. 3.

30. See, for example, the remarkably positive findings of the Search Institute

Adoption is not an easy decision, but it is a loving and courageous decision that offers good prospects for the future of both birth mother and child. To be sure, a young woman who chooses adoption will face some grief as she plans to turn over the joys and responsibilities of parenting to someone else. But she can receive help and support from extended family and the church community that will encourage and equip her to make difficult decisions for the life and long-term well-being of her child.

Other difficulties related to adoption could be solved with changes in existing laws, or new laws that favor the long-term security of the child. And there are significant ways that churches can help, both in tackling the systems that hinder the placement of children in stable and loving homes, and in becoming agents of support for those who want to give and those who want to receive a child in adoption.

## The Church and Adoption

Part of the scandal of the modern church's response to abortion is the virtual absence of interest in adoption. An article entitled, "The Adoption Option, No Help From Our Church,"[31] notes that United Methodists, one of the largest mainline Protestant denominations, while active in The Religious Coalition for Reproductive Choice, offers no help to its members seeking adoptions. The author challenges that: "Instead of investing our time and money in adoption solutions, [we in the church have] been up to our steeples in politics. . . . We should insist on the creation of an interdenominational network to help United Methodists who want to adopt children who might otherwise be abandoned or aborted."[32]

Indeed, the policies of mainline Protestant denominations do more to hinder than to help adoptions. Because of their own pro-life convictions, some Christian adoption agencies are reluctant to place

---

study of 715 adoptive families in Peter L. Benson *et al, Growing up Adopted: A Portrait of Adolescents and Their Families* (Minneapolis, Search Institute, June 1994).

31. Steve Beard, in *Good News* (May, June 1991), p. 15.
32. Ibid., pp. 15, 17.

babies with couples who are members of mainline Protestant denominations because of denominational policies favoring abortion. Few denominations are active in adoption and those agencies associated with denominations, such as Lutheran Social Services, tend to give preference in placement of the limited number of children available to members of their own denomination.

The Presbyterian Church (USA) offers no substantive help to member couples seeking to adopt, or to member birth mothers planning for the adoption of their unborn children. In recent years, however, one of its Children's Homes has begun to provide adoption services, but the effort goes virtually unacknowledged by the denomination's bureaucracy.

The church's active involvement could vastly improve the prospects for adoption in our country. Local churches could counsel young women toward adoption as an alternative to either abortion or single parenthood. The Olaskys found that when adoption is even mentioned in counseling, the incidence of women choosing it rises markedly. But the Christian church could do much better than simply to mention adoption as an option. It could give its hearty endorsement to adoption as a way of prospering the lives of all concerned.

Churches ought to recognize the adoption of a child in the same or similar way as it recognizes the birth of children in the congregation. The rose on the communion table, a common practice in many churches to observe the birth of a new baby into the community, is applicable also to adoption. Baby showers would serve as a similar community ritual, expressing joy for and acceptance of an adopted child.

Denominations could become involved themselves in providing adoption services as well as information and education on adoption. The Christian church could actively explore the hindrances to adoption and seek both legal and social means to encourage the placement of children in loving and secure homes.

There are scattered efforts that have met with success, but the church has the means to do much more. One family's testimony in a 1991 "Dear Abby" column shows the fruit of commitment that the church could replicate a thousand times over.

> . . . In 1963, my father died, leaving my mother with seven children under 15. (I'm the eldest.) Mom then adopted two war-

wounded paraplegic Vietnamese boys. Then there were nine. In 1970, Mom married the handsome Bob DeBolt, who had a daughter from a previous marriage. Then there were 10.

Mom and Bob then adopted 10 more children — most were multi-handicapped. Then there were 20. All have been raised to be totally self-sufficient. (A 16th grandchild is on the way!)

But that's not the end of the story. Mom and Dad also founded and still head a national non-profit adoption program called AASK America (Aid to Adoption of Special Kids), which places so-called "unadoptable" children with loving permanent families and charges the parents no fees! Thus, many drug-addicted children, fetal alcohol syndrome infants, children with AIDS, and scores of older abused, abandoned children throughout this country were able to celebrate the Christmas holidays with their forever families.

The "one-plus-seven" beginnings of our family have currently resulted in approximately "one-plus 7,000" adoptions of children with special needs. . . .[33]

An African-American priest, Father George Clements, adopted an African-American child and started a One Child One Church movement among African-American churches in the mid-1980s. The objective is for at least one couple in each congregation to adopt a black child, with the commitment of the whole congregation to support that family. That effort has had success in reducing the numbers of African-American children in long term foster care.

In at least ninety-five percent of the 1.5 million cases of abortion each year, there is no suspicion that the unborn child may be anything but completely healthy. Their births would be welcomed by prospective adoptive parents. But even children with serious handicaps are not unadoptable. The Christian church could make a significant difference in the lives of needy children and in the lives of childless couples longing for a family through its public voice and private counsel, and by becoming active in promoting and providing adoption services.

33. "Adoption Service Matches Special Kids," *Minneapolis Tribune*, Jan. 27, 1991.

## The Option of Single Parenthood

Though the cards are stacked against the success of single parenthood as a general rule, the church can make the difference in many cases between success and disaster for singles who parent a child alone. Some states allow for single parent adoptions, and many women are consciously choosing to have a child and remain single. Other women are single parents because they have chosen not to abort their children and, for one reason or another, also have not chosen adoption. And some women have become single parents through divorce, desertion, or death of a spouse. Natural extended families can provide immeasurable stability in these situations and the church also can be a community that becomes family to them as well, in the intimacy of personal relationships as well as in the actions of the corporate body. The influence of stable families in the congregation as active participants in the lives of children without father or mother, can go a long way toward filling the gap, providing accountability as well as tangible help, and can model a future life for those children. The church should be the body that assures that no single person has to "go it alone."

For example, one role that can be filled by local churches and that is desperately needed in our time is the education of young men for Christian family life and responsibility. Men in a local church congregation can be wonderful role models for the church's children. Nurseries and Sunday schools should have men as well as women teachers. Choirs could use a lot of tenor and bass voices. Couples can sponsor youth groups and talk to them about Christian family life and the indispensable role that fathers play. For children of households headed by women in the congregation, men can invite the children to engage in sports or other social activities. Those contacts may lead to opportunities for godly counsel, and always lead to important influence on the shaping of the lives of those children.

## Organizing to Help

Churches that understand baptism as the welcome of children into the community of believers, to whom they make their pledge of service, need a plan for how that pledge will be carried out in the lives of those children over the years. A church that wants to offer substantive and ongoing help to women and families in the variety of crisis pregnancy situations that may arise would be wise to appoint a committee with responsibility for organizing and identifying the resources of the church. In that way the church would have a designated group to provide for the education and preparation of members on an ongoing basis, to keep current on the referral resources in the community, and to update the resources of people and talents within the congregation so that crisis needs can be met quickly, and without hesitation.

That group can itself be the nucleus of the congregation's service ministry, serving as well as organizing the gifts and talents of the body. They can help the church take initiatives in outreach. They can prepare themselves to make presentations in local colleges or public and private schools where abortion counseling is otherwise common and the unmarried pregnancy rate is high. They can find ways to notify young women in crisis of their group's availability and willingness to help.[34] A church in Tulsa, Oklahoma, advertises their help in local high school newspapers, including a phone number. When a teen calls, typically she will find herself talking with one of the pastors of that church. And follow–up tangible help is available instantly from their pregnancy care committee.

The committee can help the local church prepare to observe Sanctity of Human Life Sunday at some time during the church year, when the thrust of the Sunday morning program, including the worship service, emphasizes the Christian commitment to preserve and nurture human life. It can encourage the preaching and teaching ministry of the church to include moral instruction and the church's offer to help, and can develop or compile resources for the church's library and education programs.

When a crisis arises, the committee can serve to locate the help that is needed: a home, a counselor, a baby shower, maternity clothes, a doctor, a pastor, a friend.

The committee can also help to reinforce biblical values in the lives of the church's youth. It can assure that families caring for hand-

34. Presbyterians Pro-Life, a renewal organization of members of the Presbyterian Church (USA), for example, publishes an attractive booklet entitled "Pregnant? We'll Help!" designed for churches that want to offer help to pregnant teens.

icapped and infirm family members have tangible help from the church community. The committee members can serve to integrate the gifts of the church to meet the needs that exist, and can be themselves not only organizers, but also caregivers, demonstrating that

> . . . inasmuch as you have done it unto the least of these my brothers, you have done it unto me. (Matt. 25:40 KJV)

## Resources for Locating Helping Agencies

There are community pregnancy care centers in most urban centers and in many small communities as well. International Life Services, Inc. publishes a resource directory which includes "hotline only, crisis counseling, professional counseling, post abortion service, post delivery service, adoption agency, sheltering and maternity home" and "medical services," which it revises regularly. The address is 2606½ West 8th Street, Los Angeles, CA 90057-3810.

For information on adoption and adoption agencies, including special needs adoptions, contact the National Council For Adoption, 1930 17th Street, N.W., Washington, DC 20009-6207.

# *Epilogue*

Abortion is destroying one and one-half million of God's children every year — children whom God has created to glorify him and enjoy him forever; children who do not finally belong to us but to the heavenly Father who created them and who has a plan for their future. But the lives of those children have been entrusted to us to guard and bring forth and nurture. God wants those children to be baptized into his church and to sit at his table and to be guided throughout their lives by his Word. God wants those children to be members of his universal family, the church, knowing the abundance of supporting love and Christian joy in his household and the certainty of eternal life in his kingdom. If the Christian Church will truly be the church, exhibiting the marks of the Word rightly preached about abortion; if the church will rightly administer its sacraments as contradictions of abortion's creed; if the body of Christ will properly exercise its discipline to prevent abortion and to lead those who have sanctioned and those who have had abortions to repentance and transformation of life, and if the church will properly exercise its role as the servant of Christ and of others; then we have reason to hope that the Medical Waste truck will make fewer stops at the abortion clinic. God's affirmation of life and not death in the resurrection of his Son can once again become that of the church. And thousands of voices can be raised in praise; "I am not my own! O thanks be to the God and Father of our Lord Jesus Christ! I am not my own, but his!"

# The Biology
# of the Unborn Child:
# Implications for Abortion

Thomas A. Miller, M.D.
*Department of Surgery*
*University of Texas Medical School, Houston*

Although scriptural authority must always be the standard by which decision making occurs for the Christian, it is noteworthy that recent advances in medicine and our understanding of reproduction and the biology of the unborn child support, rather than challenge, the uniqueness of unborn life. This uniqueness is especially germane to the abortion issue and individuals plagued with problem pregnancies. This uniqueness carries with it certain ethical considerations that can be discussed under the three broad headings considered below.

*Minutes,* 1992, Part I, pp. 380-383, of the Presbyterian Church (U.S.A.). This material was taken from the Minority Report of the Special Committee on Problem Pregnancies and Abortion. It was not adopted by the 204th General Assembly (1992). Used by permission.

# The Uniqueness of the Zygote[1]

It is a well established biologic fact that human life begins when an ovum (unfertilized egg) is penetrated by a sperm. This process of fertilization, technically called conception, occurs as a result of sexual intercourse in which millions of sperm are deposited into the female vagina and make their way through the uterus into the fallopian tube, where union with an ovum, newly released from the ovary, usually occurs. The fertilized egg resulting from this union, called a zygote, possesses all the hereditary material necessary to control that individual's growth and development for the rest of his or her life. Deoxyribonucleic acid, or DNA, represents the biochemical material housing this heredity. Half of this material, in the form of twenty-three chromosomes, is provided by the mother and the other half by the father, so that the zygote contains a total of forty-six chromosomes.

Each of the chromosomes is made up of a multiplicity of hereditary subunits, known as genes. Through a recently developed technique, known as "gene mapping," it has been estimated that each human chromosome individually contains as many as 1000 to 2000 gene subunits. Of the 50,000 to 100,000 genes existing in each human zygote, the various combinations that may result therefrom have been calculated to be in the billions. One observer[2] has noted that a single thread of DNA from a human zygote contains information equivalent to a library of 1000 volumes, or 600,000 printed pages with 500 words on a page. Thus, the genetic information stored in this zygote at the time of conception is equivalent to fifty times the amount of information contained in the *Encyclopedia Britannica*. Recent findings from gene mapping suggest that these estimates may even be on the low side.

1. B. T. Heffernan, "The Early Biography of Everyman," *Abortion and Social Justice,* ed. T. W. Hilgers and D. J. Horan (New York: Sheed and Ward, Inc., 1972), pp. 3-25; A. Hellegens, "Fetal Development," *Contemporary Issues in Bioethics,* ed. T. L. Beauchamp (Encino, California: Dickenson, 1978), pp. 194-199; A. W. Liley, "The Foetus in Control of His Environment," *Abortion and Social Justice,* pp. 27-36; B. Rensberger, "Creating the Ultimate Map of Our Genes," *The World Book Annual Science Supplement* (Chicago: World Book, 1989), pp. 159-171; L. B. Shettles and D. Rorvik, *Rites of Life* (Grand Rapids: Zondervan, 1983).

2. R. Houwink, *Data: Mirrors of Science* (New York: American Elsevier Publishing Co., 1970), pp. 104-190.

It is this vast amount of genetic information contained in the zygote that determines each individual's unique physical characteristics, such as the color of hair and eyes, height, and overall body build. Of further note, even before the zygote undergoes its first cell division to produce two cells, the sex of the individual has already been determined. Thus, at conception, human life is conferred and makes that life one of a kind. In view of the literally billions of combinations that may occur from the thousands of genes existent in each zygote, it is unlikely that there will ever be another zygote produced with exactly the same genetic makeup. In short, this means that there will never be another "you." Even in the case of identical twins, in which the initially formed zygote splits into two cells that somehow separate and ultimately produce two whole individuals with an identical genetic heritage, the twins are not entirely identical. Their fingerprints can be distinguished from each other as can their personalities, despite the fact that their gene makeup is identical.

Neither the sperm nor the egg possesses unique, independent human life and thus contraception in marriage for birth control purposes is not destroying human life. Unless fertilization takes place, both the sperm and the egg will die, the egg within twenty-four hours and the sperm within thirty-six to seventy-two hours. It is only the zygote that possesses true independent life, the power for self-directed growth and development, and the power of full differentiation into what we define in terms of outward appearances as a fully developed human being. All that is needed for such growth, development, and differentiation to occur is sufficient time and adequate nourishment in the form of oxygen and nutrients.

Such being the case, two fallacies need to be noted that frequently appear as established facts in the abortion literature, especially with respect to downplaying the uniqueness of the zygote. The first is the "continuum of life" notion, in which all of life is viewed as a continuum and thus the sperm and unfertilized egg are looked upon as being just as important to the human life process as the zygote itself. This view states that since the zygote is not a fully formed human being, it simply possesses the potential for life, and thus should in no way be viewed as having any particular distinctness or uniqueness. This is a completely flawed biologic notion since neither the egg nor sperm possesses the capacity for independent life in and of itself. Only the zygote resulting from the combination of chromosomes contributed from the sperm and egg begins a truly human life. Contrary to what many think, the zygote does not later become human life, nor is it potential human life; rather, it is human life, and the genetic material that it contains defines human life for the individual that has resulted from the fertilization process.

The second, equally untrue notion is that the unborn child is merely "part of the mother's body" and thus it is her right to determine whether that part can be disposed of, as she would when determining whether some body part should be removed because of infection, cancer, or for cosmetic purposes. Not only is the new life resident in the mother genetically distinct from her from the time of conception, but the unborn child also possesses separate body systems that function totally independently of the mother (i.e. circulatory, nervous, hematopoietic, endocrine, and so forth). From a biological standpoint, the mother serves to provide a source of nutrients so that the zygote can fully grow, develop, and differentiate in the full expression of its genetic capacity. If it were possible to provide such nutrients through some other source, there is every reason to believe that such processes could proceed without the necessity of the female womb and its placenta.

## Developmental Considerations with Special Emphasis on the Nervous System[3]

Shortly after its formation, the zygote divides into two cells. These two cells divide into four, the four into eight, the eight into sixteen, and so

3. R. M. Bergstrom, "Development of EEG and Unit Electrical Activity of the Brain During Ontogeny, *Ontogenesis of the Brain,* ed. L. J. Jilek and T. Stanislav (Czechoslovakia: University of Karlova Press, 1968), pp. 61-71; J. C. Birnholz, J. C. Stephens, and M. Faria, "Fetal Movement Patterns: A Possible Means of Defining Neurologic Development Milestones in Utero," *American Journal of Roentgenology* 130 (1978), pp. 540-573; R. J. Ellingson and H. R. Guenter, "Ontogenesis of the Electroencephalogram," *Development Neurology,* ed. W. A. Himwich (Springfield, Ill: Charles C. Thomas, 1970), pp. 441-474; J. M. Goldenring, "The Bring-Life Theory: Towards a Consistent Biological Definition of Humanness," *Journal of Medical Ethics* 11 (1985), pp. 198-204; H. Hamlin, "Life or Death by EEG," *Journal*

forth. These initial cell divisions take place in the fallopian tube, where fertilization usually occurs. It is not until six or seven days later that this new human life enters the uterus where implantation into the uterine lining occurs. One portion of this sphere of cells, known as the trophoblast, directly penetrates the uterine lining and develops into the placenta. The remaining part continues to develop as the embryonic human being.

The placenta is an extension of the unborn child's body and not the mother's. Almost immediately after its formation, the placenta starts producing hormones that are thrust into the mother's circulation to prevent the onset of menstruation and to bring about those other changes necessary to nurture this newly formed life. It is the newly formed human being who effects these important physiological changes, ensuring that an appropriate environment is established to enable its growth and development within the mother.

Before the first month of life is over, the embryo (as this new life is called after the second week of development) has already formed a beating heart as well as the foundations of its nervous system, including the brain, nerves, and spinal cord. So rapid is development in the first month of life, as one cell becomes millions, that all the major structures of the body are in evidence in rudimentary form by the thirtieth day. Within six weeks of conception, the nervous system is so well-developed that the muscular movements of the child are coordinated by it, despite the fact that the mother may not perceive such movements. By the sixth week the heart is complete and its heartbeat is much what it will be like in adult life. By the eighth or tenth week, the brain and lungs are largely complete in their development. Limb buds are present between four and five weeks following conception and the extremities are basically complete by the eighth or tenth week. The fingerprints that are uniquely this child's own are usually present by twelve weeks.

*of the American Medical Association* 190 (1964), pp. 112-114; N. Herschkowitz, "Brain Development in the Fetus, Neonate, and Infant," *Biol. Neonate* 54 (1988), pp. 1-19; A. W. Liley, "The Foetus in Control"; B. N. Nathanson and R. N. Ostling, *Abortion America* (Garden City, N.Y.: Doubleday), 1979; L. B. Shettles and D. Rovik, *Rites of Life*; T. Verny and J. Kelly, *The Secret Life of the Unborn Child* (New York: Summit Books, 1981), pp. 196-197; Ad Hoc Committee of Harvard Medical School on irreversible coma (1968); Guidelines for Determination of Death (1981).

By the end of the first trimester, the fetus (the technical designation given to this child from the tenth week of development until birth) can react to touch, turn its head, kick its legs, flex its wrists, make fists, and even curl its toes. Thumb sucking is fully in evidence at this point and has been observed on ultrasound movies as early as eight weeks. By the end of the twelfth week, the fetus is about three inches long and weighs one ounce. The tiny human being at this point in its development possesses almost all of the basic apparatus it will need to get through the remainder of its life. The second and third trimesters are, for the most part, the biological "finishing school," enabling the fetus to grow and develop sufficiently so that it can cope with life outside the world of the womb.

Before it was possible to observe by ultrasound the development of the live baby in the womb, the movements of the baby, perceived subjectively by the mother and called "quickening" (usually between the fourth and fifth months), were considered to mark the point at which the baby was really alive. But H. M. I. Liley, a world-renowned expert on the biology of the developing fetus, and a recognized leader in the discipline of fetal medicine, notes that "quickening" denotes nothing of the kind:

> Historically, quickening was supposed to delineate the time when the fetus became an independent human being possessed of a soul. Now, however, we know that while he may have been too small to make his motions felt, the unborn child is active and independent long before his mother feels him. Quickening is a maternal sensitivity and depends on the mother's own fat, the position of the placenta, and the size and strength of the unborn child. Quickening is hardly an objective basis for making a decision about the existence or the value of the life of the unborn child.[4]

Especially pertinent to any discussion of the abortion issue is the early development of the child's nervous system. Specialists in fetal medicine have shown clearly that the fetal brain is fully functioning by eight weeks of age. This is especially important to realize, since the current definitive and final measure of the end of human life is brain

---

4. H. M. I. Liley, *Modern Motherhood* (New York: Random House, 1969), pp. 37-38.

death, which happens when there is irreversible cessation of total brain function. The so-called Harvard criteria, established by a committee of the Harvard Medical School in 1968 to define death, would, if applied to the fetus, reveal a living human being. The Harvard criteria state that death is determined by four things: (1) lack of response to external stimuli; (2) lack of deep reflex action; (3) lack of spontaneous movement and respiratory effort; and (4) lack of brain activity as ascertained by the electroencephalogram (EEG). The developing fetus exhibits none of these "lacks" well before the conclusion of the first trimester and, many scientists would agree, as early as the eighth week. Thus, by the Harvard criteria, the fetus is sufficiently "alive and kicking" so that, were it an adult, it would be treated by every effort available to keep it alive. Responses to external stimuli, for example, have been recorded on ultrasound film as early as day thirty-six. Deep reflex action is definitely intact by day forty-two and spontaneous movements and respiratory efforts have been identified as early as the sixth week. Brain waves have been recorded as early as forty days on the electroencephalogram. In fact, the embryonic brain has now been shown to exhibit electrical patterns similar to those seen in adults, in both sleeping and waking states and in other states of consciousness produced with various drugs.

As Dr. Hannibal Hamlin of the Harvard Medical School has noted: "At any early prenatal stage of life, the EEG reflects a distinctly individual pattern that soon becomes truly personalized."[5] And Verney and Kelley have observed: "The fact that the unborn test alive by all four criteria (of brain function) raises significant questions about our current attitudes toward abortion."[6] Since the taking of human life post-birth would be considered murder if brain function was intact by the Harvard criteria, it seems strange indeed that destroying the fetus by abortion after two months of development is considered acceptable even though the fetus at this stage of life has been shown to be a living human being by our current definitions of life and death.

5. H. Hamlin, "Life or Death."
6. T. Verny and J. Kelly, *Secret Life,* pp. 196-197.

## The Changing Definition of Viability and Its Relation to Humanness[7]

Viability is that stage of fetal development when the unborn child is potentially capable of living outside the womb of the mother (i.e. can survive), albeit with artificial help. This term has frequently been used as a measure of humanness. In actual fact, viability is simply the measure of the sophistication of available life-support systems. For example, twenty-five years ago it was highly unlikely that a child born at thirty weeks following conception would survive. Not only do babies born at thirty weeks commonly survive today, but sufficient numbers of cases are now available to indicate that babies born at twenty weeks of age have a reasonable degree of likelihood of surviving.

What has changed over this twenty-five year period has been the development of better life support systems around the baby as well as doctors and nurses who have devoted their lives to managing premature infants so that the baby can have a "fighting chance" of making it. Only a few years ago, such an accomplishment would have been considered next to impossible. Many specialists in fetal medicine have even predicted that eventually it will be possible successfully to maintain babies weighing half a pound or even less outside the womb.

Since prematurely born infants can now be supported successfully so that survival is often possible, it seems strange that such a baby is treated as a fully human being with all the rights and privileges attendant thereto when born prematurely, but such human rights do not supervene if a baby of similar age is chosen to be aborted by its mother. For example, what makes a prematurely born twenty-five-week-old baby a human, and, if intentionally destroyed after birth, a victim of murder, when another baby of a similar age is aborted and murder is not considered an issue? How does birth change the status of these two babies? Does birth define humanness? Hardly!

Most certainly the age at which a premature infant is likely to survive will continue to decrease as our knowledge of fetal physiology becomes more sophisticated. Some specialists in fetal medicine are

7. Nathanson and Ostling, *Abortion America;* Shettles and Rorvik, *Rites of Life;* Dr. and Mrs. J. C. Willke, *Abortion: Questions and Answers* (Cincinnati, Ohio: Hayes Publishing Co., 1988), pp. 33-73.

already envisioning a day when "artificial wombs" will be available to provide the proper nutrients and nourishment to enable the developing fetus to reach a point of independent existence, regardless of when it is born. Does the definition of humanness change because a child developed outside of the womb rather than in it? Or is the human being really existent from the moment an egg is fertilized by a sperm and thus has nothing to do with some predetermined age after conception? In light of the scientific facts, the answers are obvious.